JILL LIVETT JACINTA O'LEARY MARK TORY

TECH *by* DESIGN

WORKBOOK

FOR THE VICTORIAN CURRICULUM

Tech by Design Workbook
1st Edition
Jill Livett
Jacinta O'Leary
Mark Tory

Publishing editor: Sam Bonwick
Project editor: Mandy Herbet
Editor: Sabita Naheswaran
Proofreader: Monica Schaak
Permissions researcher: Helen Mammides
Production controller: Emma Roberts
Cover design: Watershed Design
Text design: Watershed Design
Cover images: Getty Images/Paper Boat Creative, Getty Images/Colin Anderson, Shutterstock.com/ildogesto
Typeset by: Q2A Media

Any URLs contained in this publication were checked for currency during the production process. Note, however, that the publisher cannot vouch for the ongoing currency of URLs.

For product information and technology assistance,
in Australia call **1300 790 853**;
in New Zealand call **0800 449 725**

For permission to use material from this text or product, please email
aust.permissions@cengage.com

ISBN 978 0 17 040020 6

Cengage Learning Australia
Level 7, 80 Dorcas Street
South Melbourne, Victoria Australia 3205

Cengage Learning New Zealand
Unit 4B Rosedale Office Park
331 Rosedale Road, Albany, North Shore 0632, NZ

For learning solutions, visit **cengage.com.au**

Printed in China by 1010 Printing International Limited.
5 6 7 25 24 23

CONTENTS

9780170400206

ABOUT THIS BOOK

Working with *Tech by Design*

Tech by Design is a comprehensive resource addressing the knowledge, understanding, processes and production skills required of Design and Technologies students, as defined in the Victorian Curriculum levels 7–10.

The *Tech by Design* Workbook is split into three parts – part one focuses on understanding the design process and key knowledge for the materials and technologies specialisations, engineering principles and systems, and food and fibre production technologies contexts.

Part two takes an integrated approach and addresses the technologies and society content, as well as the processes and production skills for creating designed solutions through a series of design challenges suitable for wood, metal, plastic, textiles, modelling and prototyping. The inside front cover features a full-colour guide to which materials can be used with the challenges.

Part three provides templates for students to respond to the design challenges and build a folio of work, following the design process as defined in the Victorian Curriculum. Templates can be written directly into or used as a guide for students completing folios partially or entirely in digital format. Clear directions on how to use the templates are integrated into the design challenges. Opportunities for learning in STEM are spread throughout *Tech by Design*. The *Tech by Design* workbook can be used on its own or with the student text book. A teacher resources website is also available.

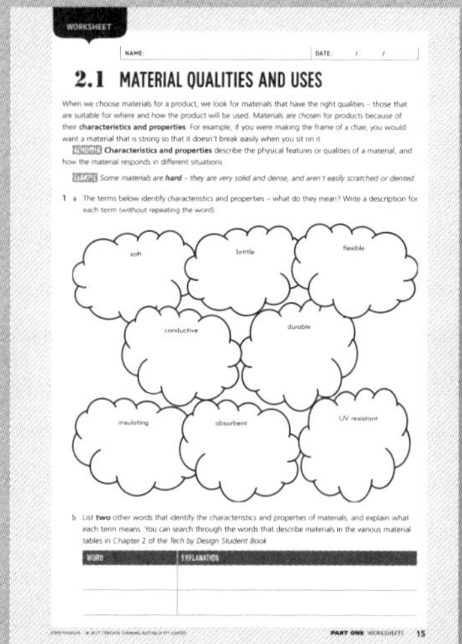
WORKSHEET

NAME: DATE: / /

2.1 MATERIAL QUALITIES AND USES

soft, brittle, flexible, conductive, durable, insulating, absorbent, UV resistant

WORD | EXPLANATION

PART ONE WORKSHEETS 15

Worksheets

Practical activities and guidance approaching learning in a fun and engaging format.

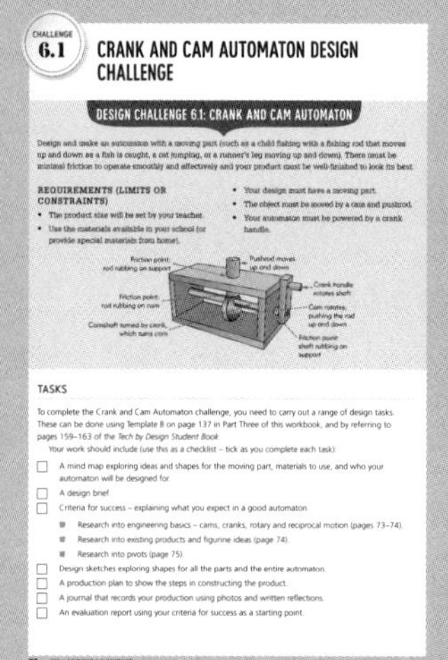
CHALLENGE 6.1 CRANK AND CAM AUTOMATON DESIGN CHALLENGE

DESIGN CHALLENGE 6.1: CRANK AND CAM AUTOMATON

REQUIREMENTS (LIMITS OR CONSTRAINTS)

TASKS

Challenges

Provides a framework for the creation of design solutions across a range of materials.

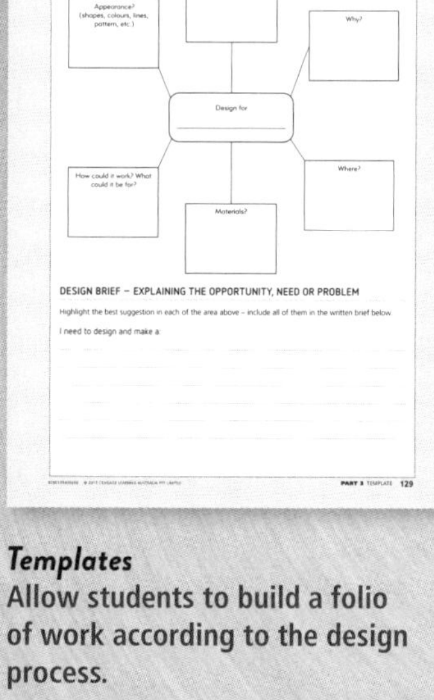
TEMPLATE A: GENERAL

NAME OF CHALLENGE:

Who? Why? Design for Where? Materials? How could it work? What could it be for?

DESIGN BRIEF – EXPLAINING THE OPPORTUNITY, NEED OR PROBLEM

I need to design and make a

PART 3 TEMPLATE 129

Templates

Allow students to build a folio of work according to the design process.

Weblinks

Students and teachers can link directly to external websites referred to in *Tech by Design* via the free, unprotected weblinks site.

Answers

Answers to selected worksheet activities.

9780170400206

WORKSHEET

NAME: DATE: / /

1.1 DESIGN PROBLEMS AND OPPORTUNITIES

DESIGN PROBLEMS

1 Listed below in the right column are some everyday products. In the column to the left, write down the problem that each product solves. The first one has been completed for you.

REMEMBER You need to describe the problem that existed before the product was designed or made. You could consider it from a personal point of view.

EXAMPLE **Problem:** *When I ride my bike to school, my shoulder bag always twists around to the front and knocks my knees.* **Possible solution:** *A wire basket to fit my bike.*

PROBLEM	THIS DESIGN/PRODUCT IS A POSSIBLE SOLUTION
Parents are physically unable to carry their infants and toddlers around with them everywhere they walk.	Stroller
	Traffic lights
	Remote control
	Sticky tape dispenser
	Giant chessboard in a community garden
	Wheel
	Beanie
	Liquid paper
	Sunglasses
	Portable light

2 List **four** products that you own and describe the 'design problem' they solve.

PRODUCT	SOLVES THE PROBLEM OF:

OPPORTUNITIES

3 You may also be asked to design a product for a situation where a solution is not yet available. This is called an opportunity. Some possible future opportunities are listed below. Think of **three** more future opportunities that you or your classmates could design for.

A FUTURE OPPORTUNITY THAT I SEE IS:
Designing a cover for a battery that stores solar power for a house
Designing bicycle jackets with lights controlled by cuff buttons to switch them on and off, to indicate turns, etc.
Designing a lock-up box for the street for shared car use

WORKSHEET

1.2 THE DESIGN PROCESS

In the space below, list the activities in each step of the design process that the designer of this chair would have completed. Make the activities specific to the chair (e.g. the designer researched how to make the seat adjustable). Remember to look at the photo of the product as well as the product description.

Leander high chair H: 83 cm, W: 55 cm, D: 56 cm. Weighs only 5.1 kg. Made of moulded European beechwood. Finished with water-based lacquer. Adjustable.

Leander®

STEP	GIVE SPECIFIC EXAMPLES OF WHAT THE DESIGNER WOULD HAVE DONE AT EACH STEP
1 Investigating	
2 Generating	
3 Planning and managing	
4 Producing	
5 Evaluating	

WORKSHEET

1.3 ANALYSING A PRODUCT

Draw or attach a photo in the space at the centre of the diagram below of a product you think is 'cool'. Fill out the boxes by finishing the starter sentence relating to the corresponding instruction in the grey circle.

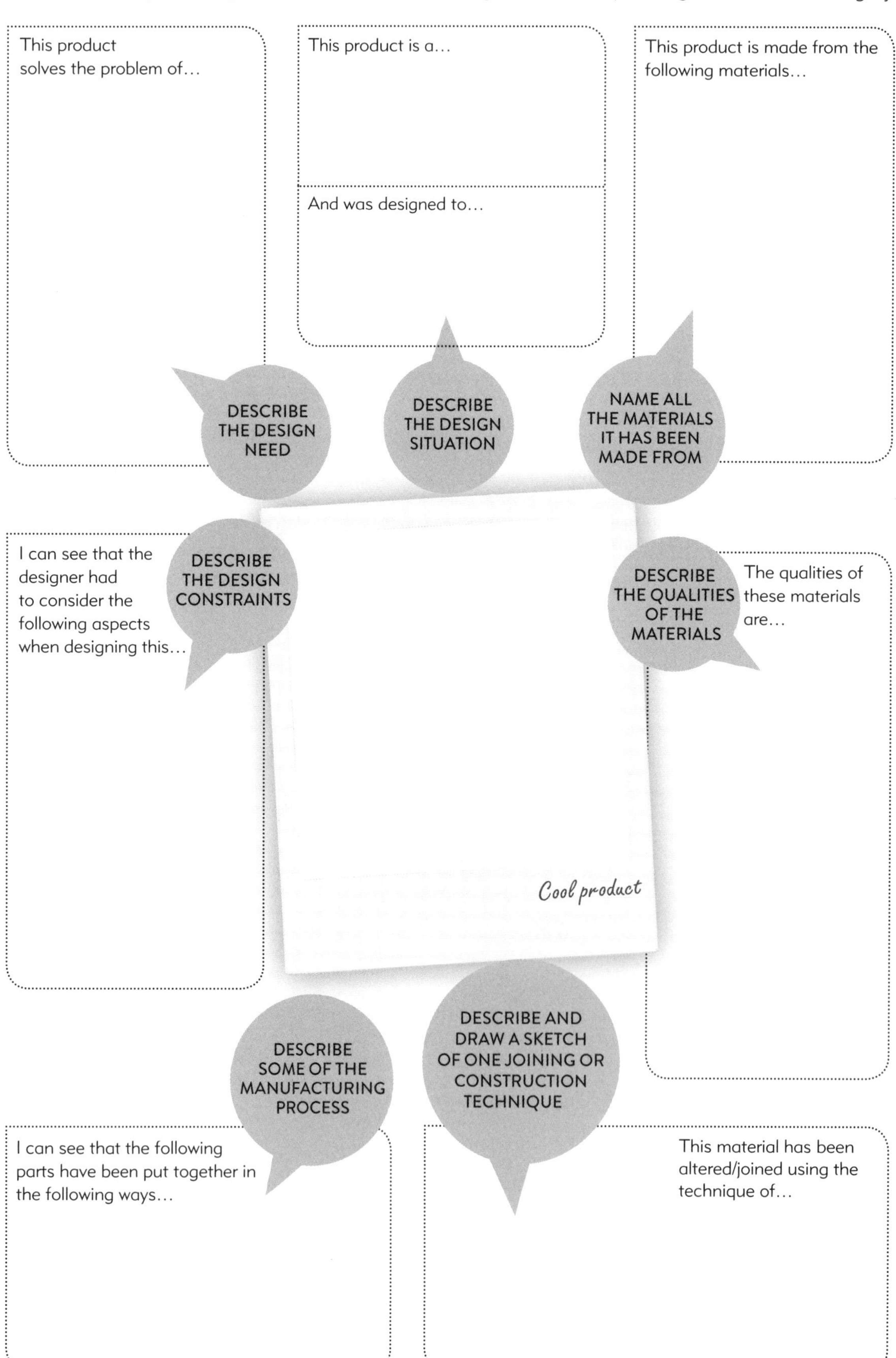

9780170400206

WORKSHEET

1.4 PMI – PLUS, MINUS, INTERESTING

This worksheet can be used to analyse a product (either a product you designed and made or someone else's) to identify what is good about it, what is interesting and what can be improved.

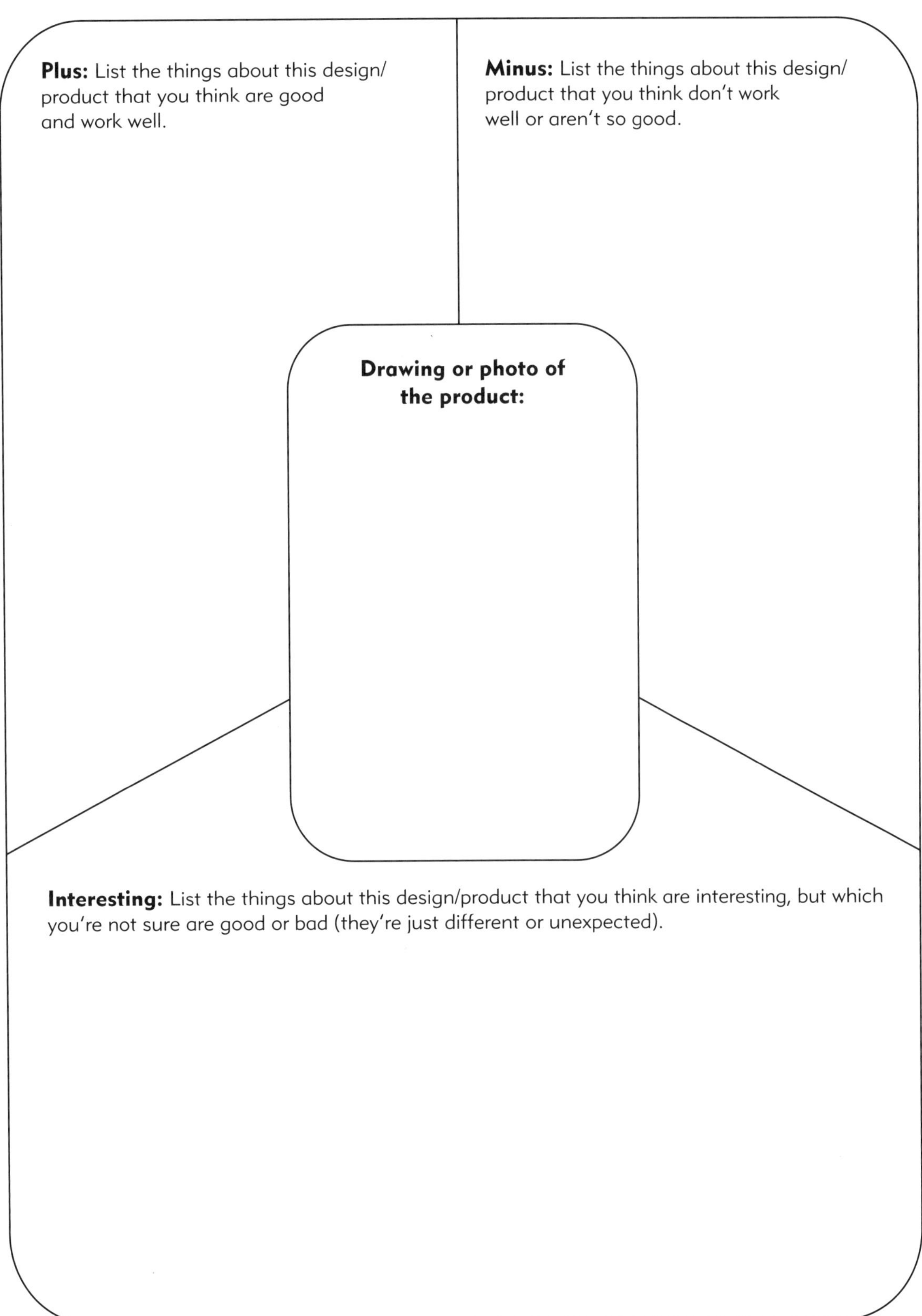

WORKSHEET

1.5 DESIGN WEB

Use this design web to assist in preparing a design brief. In the space underneath, outline any constraints or limits (as set by your teacher) relating to your design.

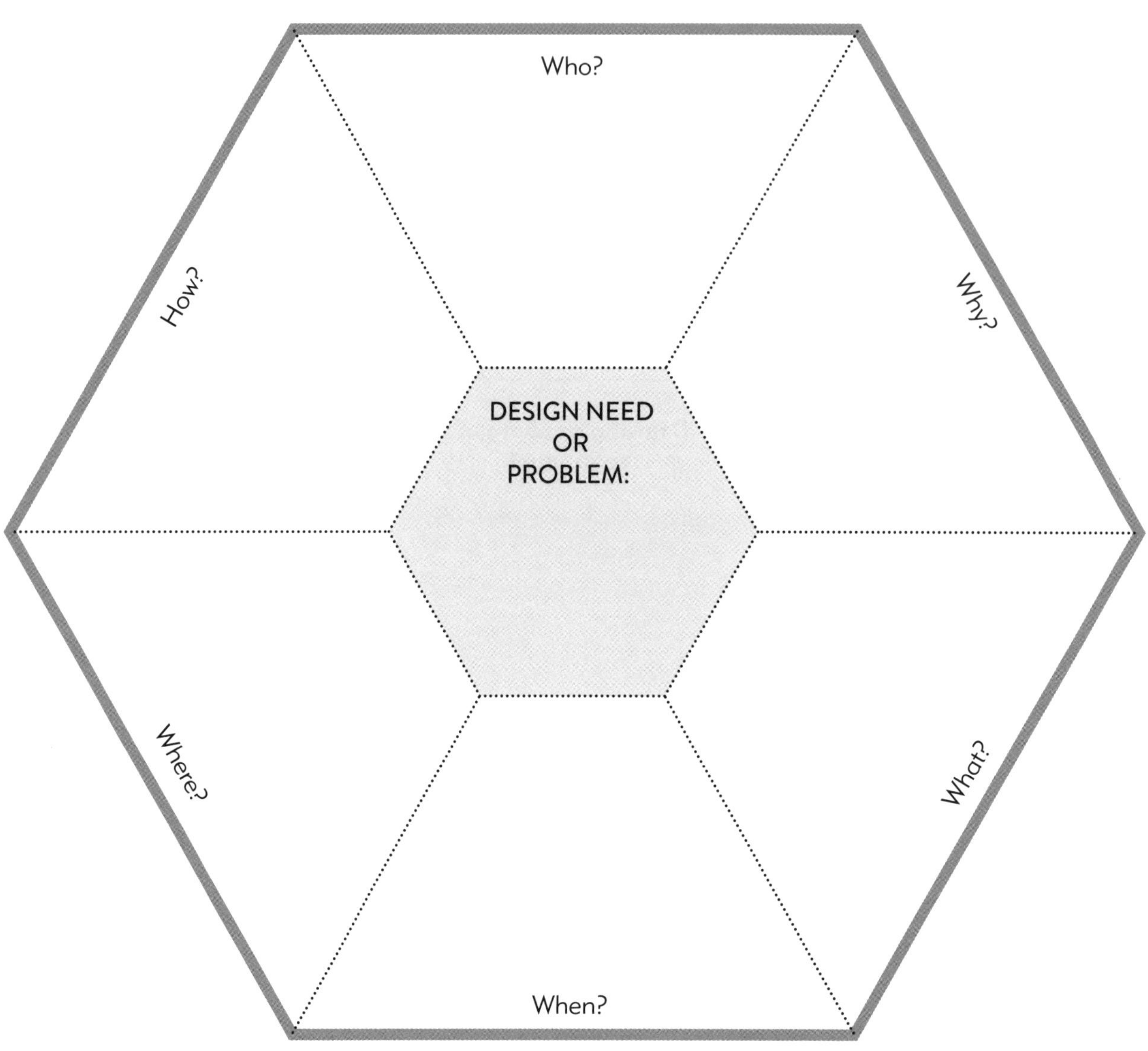

Who might use the product?

Why do they need it?

What does it need to do?

When do they need the product?

Where will it be used?

How might it work?

CONSTRAINTS OR LIMITS (SET BY YOUR TEACHER)

WORKSHEET

1.6 GRAPHIC ORGANISERS TO PLAN RESEARCH

FISHBONE DIAGRAM

Use this fishbone diagram to note down ideas for your design and what you may need to research, practise or explore. Add extra ribs and/or change their names in a new drawing if needed.

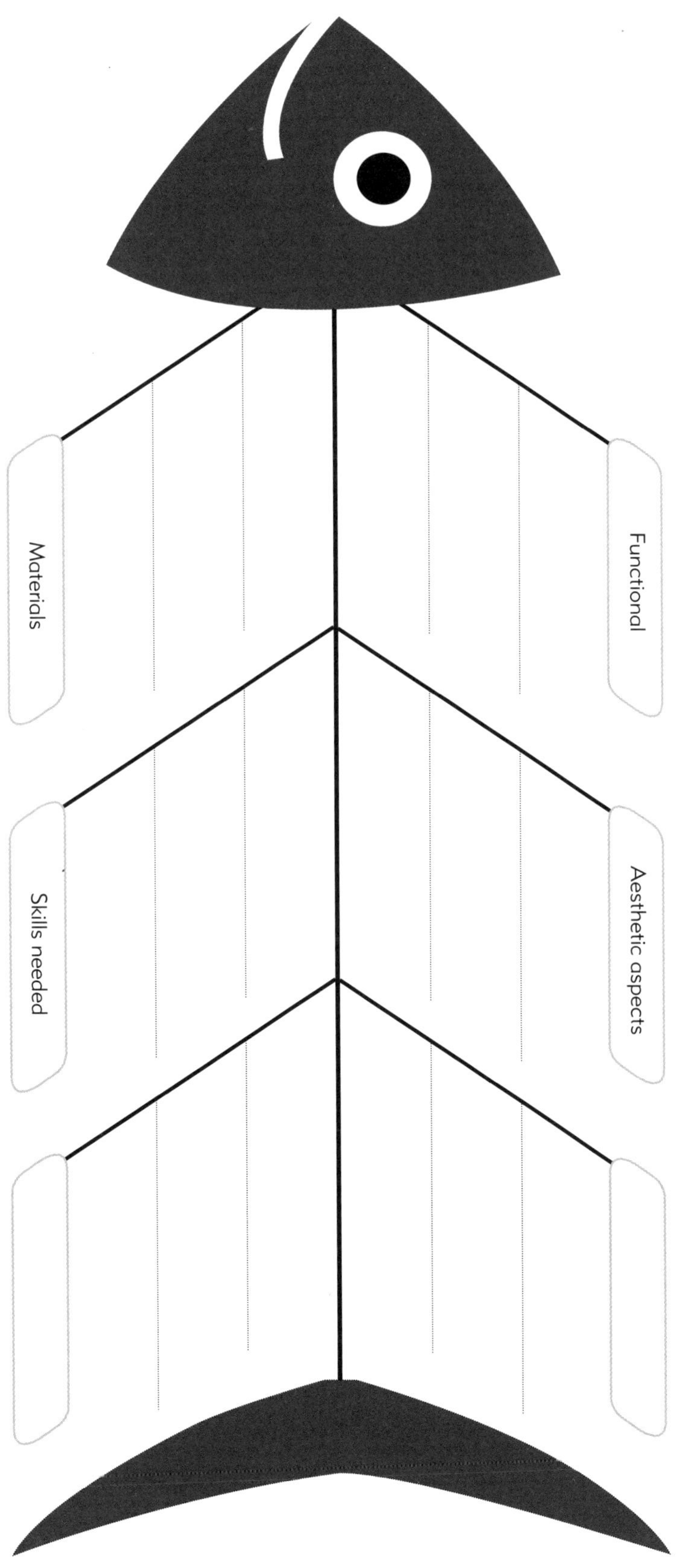

WORKSHEET

1.7 RESEARCH FOR DESIGN

PRIMARY AND SECONDARY RESEARCH

Relevant and thorough research is an important part of the design process.

The areas you should research will depend on the type of product or solution you are designing and making. Useful areas to research include:

Materials
- characteristics and properties (research and testing)
- cost

Tools and equipment
- what they are used for
- availability
- safety

Existing designs
- appearance, new ways of doing things, construction, etc.
- how they work
- future directions

The context
- finding out more about the **people** using the product (the users) and the design **situation**

Sustainability
- source of materials
- reducing waste
- ability to recycle
- alternative healthier processes

Processes
- shaping and joining techniques
- decorative methods
- finishing methods and materials
- equipment and level of skill required
- safety

Components and additional parts
- notions for textiles products
- components and parts for wood, metal and plastic products
- mechanical components – e.g. gears, wheels, etc.
- electrical and electronic components
- cost

You can find out information for yourself (**primary** source research) or you can learn from other people's investigations (**secondary** source research).

1 In each box above, list a primary or secondary research activity you could do to find out about one of the dot points in the research area (e.g. materials – check the price of timber at the local hardware store: primary).

2 a Think about how or where you would look to find useful information for the research areas listed below.

b Identify whether each source of information is primary research or secondary research.

RESEARCH AREA	HOW OR WHERE WOULD YOU FIND INFORMATION ABOUT THIS?	PRIMARY OR SECONDARY RESEARCH?
To find out if plastic materials are recyclable		
To find the strongest join for the structure you are designing		
To find a decorative technique that looks good		
To find out what other designers have created		

WORKSHEET

1.8 DESCRIBING DESIGN

DESIGN ELEMENTS AND PRINCIPLES

Design elements are the building blocks of design – the basic visual tools used to create a design. The design principles describe the way the elements are put together and organised.

1 When describing products, it's good to have a range of words to use. Fill in the spaces below with **five or six** words or phrases that describe design elements and principles. Some examples of descriptive words can be found on pages 37–43 of the *Tech by Design* Student Book. You may find it easier to refer to or look at specific products to complete this activity.

Design terms

DESIGN ELEMENTS				SOME DESIGN PRINCIPLES	
COLOUR	LINE	SHAPE	TEXTURE	BALANCE/ PROPORTION	PATTERN
Bright	Squiggly	Geometric	Furry	Even	Repeating circles

2 List and discuss **three or four** words that are used to name or describe possible materials used to make products. Also list and discuss the names of **four or five** different product styles and describe what they are like.

MATERIALS–WHAT ARE THINGS MADE OF?	WHAT DO THEY LOOK LIKE? HOW DO THEY FEEL?	STYLE	DESCRIBE WHAT EACH STYLE LOOKS LIKE
Pine, aluminium		Industrial, Gothic, country	

3 Choose **one** of the following products and write a description in the space provided (two or three sentences) that uses the words you listed in questions 1 and 2. Make sure you discuss:

- the purpose of the product or how it works
- the materials it is made from
- phrases to describe the design elements and principles that you can see (e.g. shape, colour, line, texture, proportion, etc.)
- any 'stand out' features of its appearance or style.

PRODUCT 1	PRODUCT 2	PRODUCT 3
	Imagefolk/Zoonar/Phil Crean	Getty Images/David Cooper

Description: Product number ....

....

....

....

....

....

....

....

....

....

....

....

9780170400206

WORKSHEET

1.9 DESIGN INSPIRATION AND ANALYSIS

1 Find **three** images of creative products similar to the type of product you are going to design and make. Paste your images into the boxes below.

2 For each image, write a comment that **describes** the product, explains **what you like** about the design, or describes any part of the product that might **give you ideas** for your design. Your comment needs to be two or three sentences in length. Discuss:

- how the product works, its purpose, etc. (i.e. function)
- what materials are used
- how the designer has used colour, shape, line, pattern, etc. (i.e. design elements and principles)
- the features that contribute to its overall look and style.

DESIGN 1	COMMENT:
DESIGN 2	COMMENT:
DESIGN 3	COMMENT:

WORKSHEET

1.10 DESIGN ELEMENTS

The design elements are:

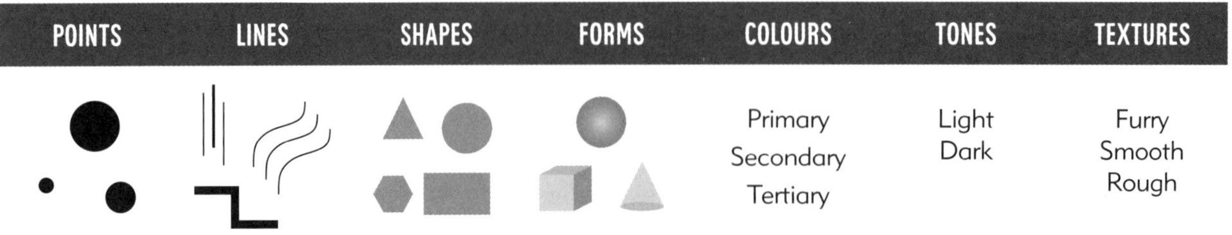

Draw at least **four** of your own examples of the design elements in the boxes below. Annotate your examples to explain how they could be included in your project.

COLOURS

POINTS

LINES

FORMS

TONES

TEXTURES

SHAPES

9780170400206

WORKSHEET

1.11 DESIGN PRINCIPLES

PRINCIPLES

- symmetry/asymmetry
- space – positive and negative
- balance
- unity
- pattern
- rhythm
- proportion
- contrast
- stability
- tension.

Choose from and combine the above principles to create **five** new designs for a teapot. See more about design principles on pages 41–43 of the *Tech by Design* Student Book.

e.g. Stability – change the balance of the teapot so it is flatter and heavier (more stable).

e.g. Proportion – change the proportions by elongating the body and lid, and narrowing the spout and handle.

e.g. Contrast – apply contrasting textures or colours to the existing teapot or to one of your new designs.

e.g. Tension – change some proportions or angles so that the teapot appears to be delicately balanced.

Choose your own combination of principles.

1.12 SUSTAINABILITY – MAPPING A PRODUCT

1 Select **one** of the products below – draw a circle around the image to indicate your choice.

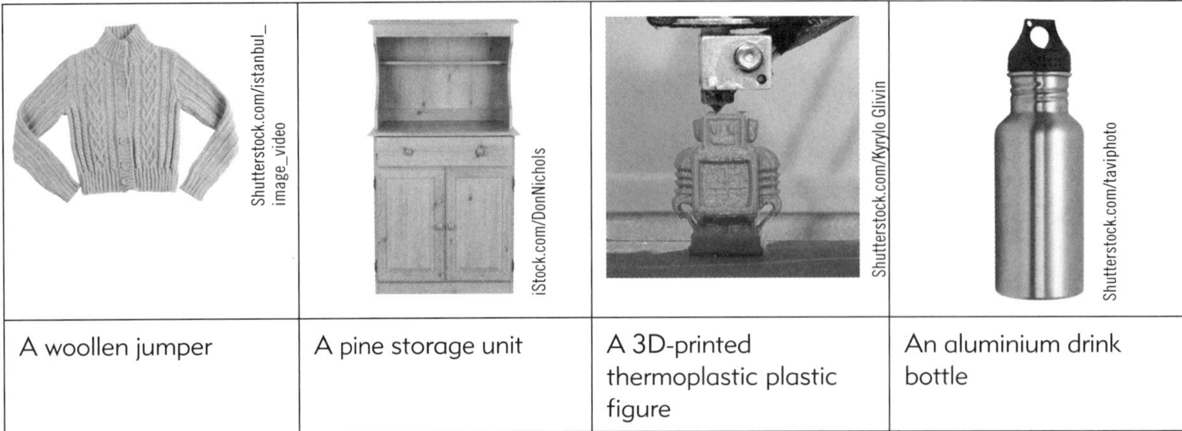

A woollen jumper	A pine storage unit	A 3D-printed thermoplastic plastic figure	An aluminium drink bottle

2 In the boxes below, **draw** a diagram that describes each stage of this product's life – from material sourcing to disposal. Identify some of the sustainability issues related to each stage.

Material sourcing and processing

Sustainability issues or concerns:

Making the product

Sustainability issues or concerns:

Transporting the product

Sustainability issues or concerns:

Using the product

Sustainability issues or concerns:

What happens to the product at the end of its useful life?

Sustainability issues or concerns:

  9780170400206

WORKSHEET

NAME: DATE: / /

2.1 MATERIAL QUALITIES AND USES

When we choose materials for a product, we look for materials that have the right qualities – those that are suitable for where and how the product will be used. Materials are chosen for products because of their **characteristics and properties**. For example, if you were making the frame of a chair, you would want a material that is strong so that it doesn't break easily when you sit on it.

REMEMBER **Characteristics and properties** describe the physical features or qualities of a material, and how the material responds in different situations.

EXAMPLE *Some materials are **hard** – they are very solid and dense, and aren't easily scratched or dented.*

1 a The terms below identify characteristics and properties – what do they mean? Write a description for each term (without repeating the word).

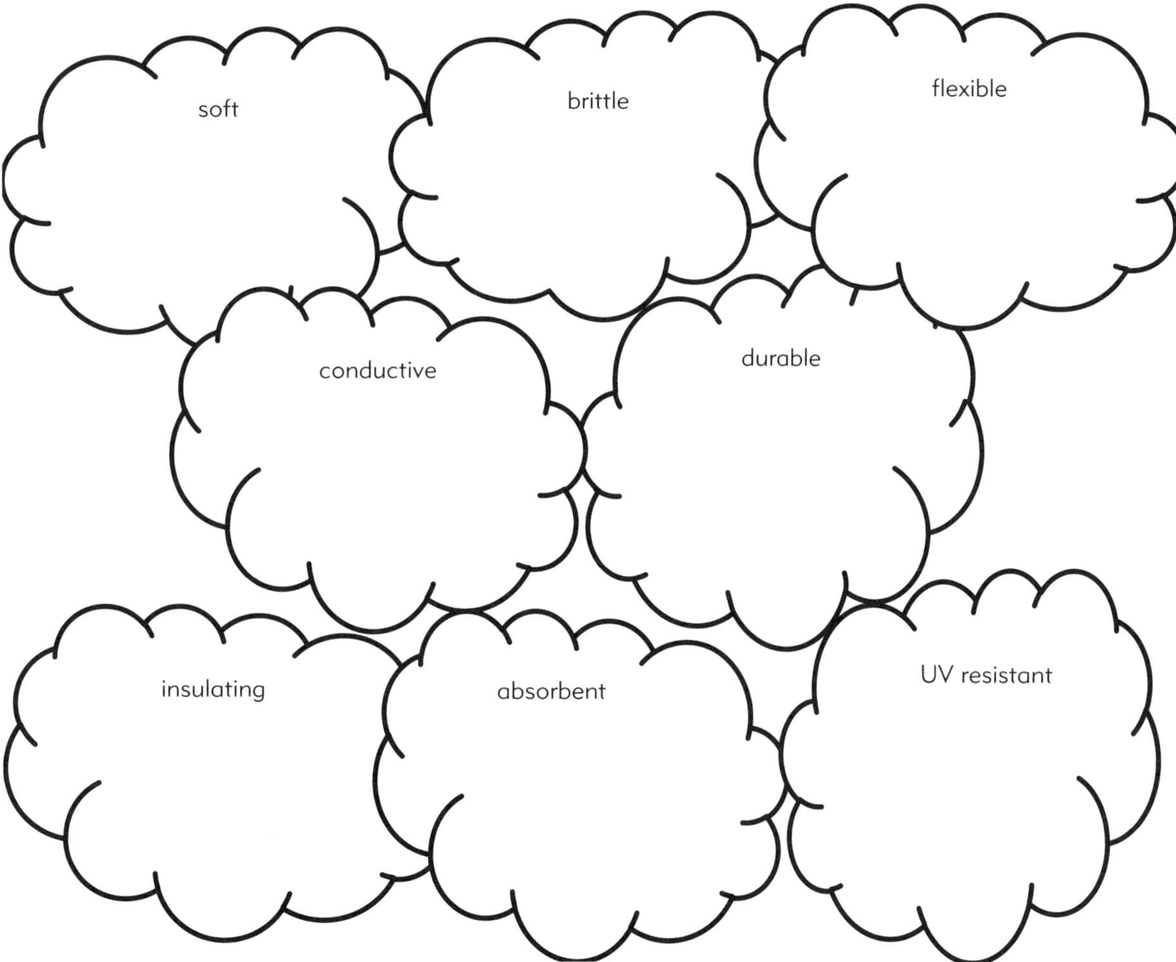

b List **two** other words that identify the characteristics and properties of materials, and explain what each term means. You can search through the words that describe materials in the various material tables in Chapter 2 of the *Tech by Design Student Book*.

WORD	EXPLANATION

2 There are a number of products shown in the following table.

- List at least **four** characteristics and properties that each product needs its materials to have.
- Identify **one or two** materials that have these characteristics and properties – materials that would be a suitable choice for this product.

PRODUCT	CHARACTERISTICS AND PROPERTIES	SUITABLE MATERIAL
Swimwear Shutterstock.com/Fereshteh		
Park bench Shutterstock.com/imnoom		
Case for a musical instrument Shutterstock.com/Elnur		

3 Sustainable materials

a When we want to choose sustainable materials to make a product, it is important that the material used has **durability**. Explain why choosing durable materials might make a product more sustainable.

....

....

b List **two** material characteristics or properties that might help products be more durable and sustainable.

i ....

ii ....

4 Find a new material on the internet – one that has been developed or invented recently and isn't commonly used. Describe this new material and its characteristics and properties, and think of two or three types of products it would be suitable for.

MATERIAL NAME: ....

DESCRIPTION	CHARACTERISTICS/PROPERTIES	USES

MATERIALS

Visit materia.nl, a website that has descriptions of many interesting materials. Alternatively, conduct an internet search for 'new materials'.

MATERIA.NL

WORKSHEET

2.2 FIBRES, FABRICS AND YARNS

To make good decisions about which fabric to choose for a textiles product, you need to know about fibres and fabrics.

1 In the textiles area, the main materials we discuss and make choices about are **fibres**, **fabrics** and **yarns**. Explain what we are talking about when we use these terms.

a Fibre: ....

b Fabric: ....

c Yarn: ....

2 The following tree diagram shows how fibres are organised and divided. List the missing categories and sub-categories, and give an example for each sub-category. (You can find information about this in the *Tech by Design Student Book* on page 51.)

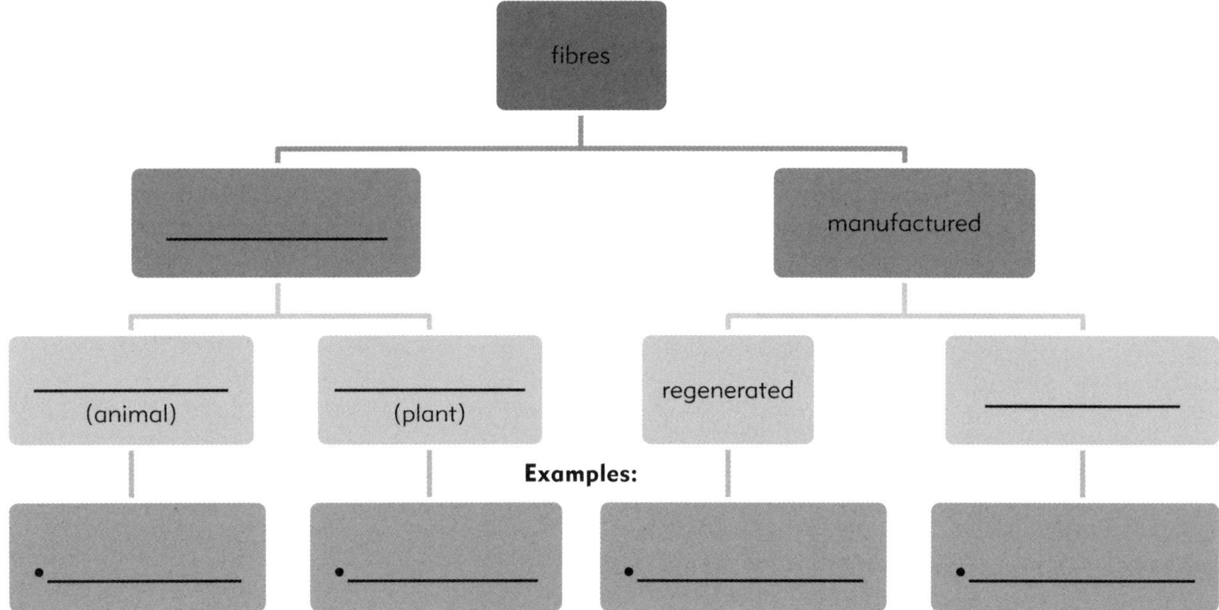

3 Explain what each of the following fibre category terms mean.

TERM	EXPLANATION
Synthetic	
Natural	
Manufactured	
Regenerated	
Cellulose	

4 Different fibres look, feel and act differently, and are used for different types of products. In the following table:

- list a specific fibre for each of these sub-categories.
- describe what each fibre is like (e.g. appearance, feel/texture, sheen, warmth, creasing).
- list at least **two** types of products (clothing and/or non-clothing) that these fibres are suitable for.

SUB-CATEGORY	FIBRE	DESCRIPTION	SUITABLE FOR THESE PRODUCTS
Natural – protein			
Natural – cellulose			
Regenerated			
Fully synthetic			

5 Choose a natural fibre such as wool, cotton, jute, hemp, silk or another. Draw a flow diagram or cartoon in the space below to show the stages a natural fibre needs to go through to be turned into a useable material, starting with its source and ending with a piece of fabric. Write comments to explain each stage.

STAGES:

COMMENTS:

FABRIC CONSTRUCTION

Fibres are put together or constructed to make fabric in different ways. The way a fabric is constructed has an impact on what the fabric is like and what it might be suitable for.

6 The following table shows diagrams of three different construction methods.

- Write the correct type of construction under each diagram – choose from the following: *felted, woven, knitted*.
- Describe what these fabrics are usually like (stiff, non-creasing, etc.).

Diagram	1 µm		
Type of construction			
Description			

FIBRES AND FABRICS IN ACTION

7 Choose your favourite piece of clothing and complete the following table.

Draw a picture of your clothing (in colour) or attach a photo.	Describe what the fabric is like.	Why do you like this piece of clothing?
	Explain when you use it.	Find out what fibre it is made from, and where it is made (this should be on the label). Fibre: Country:

8 What fibres and fabric construction would you use to make the following products?

T-shirt		**Tent**	
Shutterstock.com/Dmitry Zimin		Shutterstock.com/Mathisa	
Fibre:	Fabric:	Fibre:	Fabric:
Why?		Why?	
Beanbag cover		**Sporting clothes**	
iStock.com/4x6		Shutterstock.com/PR Image Factory	
Fibre:	Fabric:	Fibre:	Fabric:
Why?		Why?	

WORKSHEET

2.3 WOOD

1 Name the parts of the tree in the following diagram.

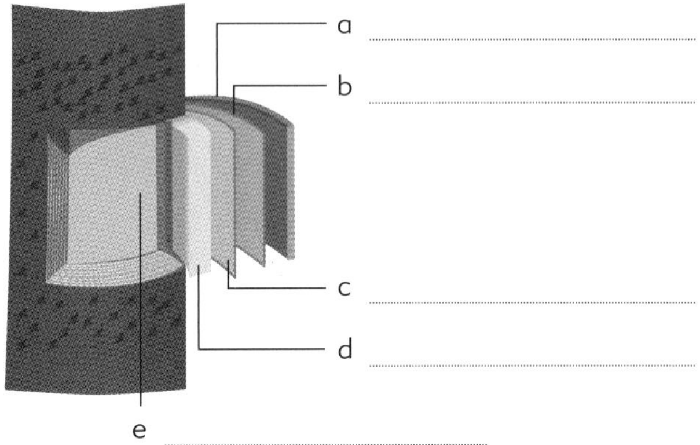

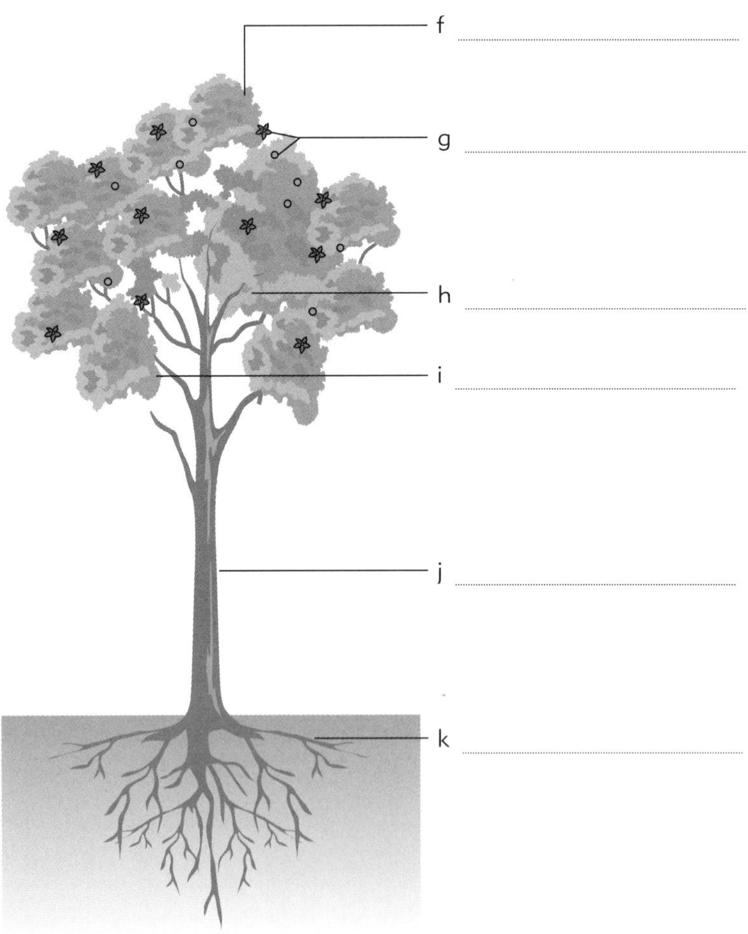

Sapwood	Roots	Cambium	Trunk
Flowers, fruit and nuts	Branches and twigs	Crown	Heartwood
Outer bark	Inner bark	Leaves and needles	

9780170400206

2 Identify the differences between softwoods and hardwoods by writing the correct option, and then give **three** examples of each type of timber.

OPTIONS	SOFTWOOD	HARDWOOD
Leaves **OR** needles?		
Flowers/fruits/ nuts **OR** cones?		
Only evergreen **OR** may lose their foliage in winter?		
Example timbers		

3 Choose **two Australian** timbers and answer the following questions.

	TIMBER 1	TIMBER 2
Common name?		
Scientific name?		
Softwood or hardwood?		
Appearance?		
Properties/ qualities?		
What types of products is it used to make?		

4 a What is the difference between a forest and a plantation?

....

b What advantages and disadvantages does each have as a material source for timber products?

....

....

5 Research and complete the information about the manufactured timbers listed below.

	HOW IS IT MADE?	WHAT PRODUCTS IS IT USED TO MAKE, OR WHERE IN A PRODUCT MIGHT IT BE USEFUL?	SUSTAINABILITY OR SAFETY ISSUES?
Plywood			
Particle board or MDF			
Blockboard			

6 Why might a manufactured board be more useful for constructing some types of products, or parts of a product? What advantages do manufactured boards have over solid timber?

....

....

7 a Is a bamboo plant classified as a tree? If not, what is it?

....

b Why is bamboo a good material to use when making products or buildings?

....

....

8 In the spaces provided, draw a picture of **four** different products/objects that are made from timber (think about transport, building, furniture, instruments, etc.). Identify the timber qualities (characteristics or properties) that are important for each product, and the types of timber that might be used to make it.

PRODUCT 1	**PRODUCT 2**
What does the timber need to be like for this product? (i.e. properties, qualities such as soft, dense)	What does the timber need to be like for this product? (i.e. properties, qualities) ....
Which timber/s would be suitable for this type of product?	Which timber/s would be suitable for this type of product? ....
PRODUCT 3	**PRODUCT 4**
What does the timber need to be like for this product? (i.e. properties, qualities)	What does the timber need to be like for this product? (i.e. properties, qualities) ....
Which timber/s would be suitable for this type of product?	Which timber/s would be suitable for this type of product? ....

soft	dense	hard	straight/even grain
figured grain	flexible	heavy/light	resistant to pests
resistant to water	easy to machine	rigid/stiff and strong	stable
stains well			

WORKSHEET

2.4 METALS

Metals are divided into the following categories.

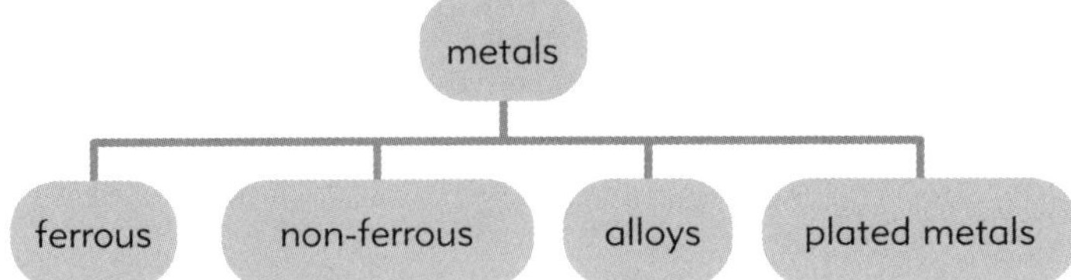

1 For each category of metal listed below:

- explain what the term means.
- think of an example and describe it.
- identify **two or three** products or parts of a product that might be made from this metal.

	EXPLANATION	EXAMPLE AND DESCRIPTION	PRODUCT USE
Ferrous			
Non-ferrous			
Alloy			
Plated metal			
Precious metal			

2 Draw a flow diagram or cartoon in the space below to show the stages metal needs to go through to become a useable material, starting with where it is sourced and ending with a piece of metal ready for production. Write comments to explain each stage.

STAGES:

COMMENTS:

3 Investigate and list the metals mined in Australia.

SUSTAINABILITY

4 a Describe some of the sustainability issues and concerns related to the processing and use of metals.

b Explain some positive actions that can reduce these environmental and social impacts.

c What is the most sustainable aspect of metals?

WORKSHEET

2.5 PLASTICS

Plastic is one of the most used materials in our society. There are many different types of plastics, and they are used to make a wide range of different products. Plastics are extremely useful, but they can also cause serious problems.

1 Approximately how many years ago were the first plastics invented?

....

2 What is the difference between thermoplastic and thermoset plastics?

....

....

3 Which of these types of plastic can be recycled?

....

PLASTIC SYMBOLS

4 a What do the symbols printed on some plastic products indicate, and why do we have them?

....

....

b Complete the following table.

Symbol	1	2	3	4	5	6
Name						
Uses						

Shutterstock.com/Baloncici

  9780170400206

ADVANTAGES AND DISADVANTAGES OF PLASTIC

5 a Complete the following table.

- In the advantages column of the table below, give three reasons why plastics are useful as a replacement for more traditional materials to make everyday products.
- In the disadvantages column, describe three problems caused by the use of plastic to make everyday products.

ADVANTAGES	DISADVANTAGES
•	•
•	•
•	•

b List three plastic products that cause significant environmental problems.

PLASTIC PRODUCT	EXPLANATION OF THE ENVIRONMENTAL PROBLEMS THEY CAUSE

c What can we do to reduce the environmental problems caused by using plastic?

6 What sort of plastic might be used for these products?

7 Collect examples of other products or objects made from plastic.

- Draw or attach photos of the products in the following table.
- Describe the plastic (e.g. soft/hard, flexible/stiff, shiny/dull, thick/thin, transparent/opaque).
- Try to identify the type of plastic it might be made from.
- Is this a product that is used once (single-use/disposable), for a short time, or for a long time (a year or more)?

Product			
Description of plastic			
Type of plastic			
Length of use			

WORKSHEET

2.6 WMP MATERIALS: TYPES AND STANDARD SIZES

There are many wood, metal and plastic materials you can use for your products. They could include some of the materials listed in the table below, and may include others. **Your teacher will show you a sample of many of the materials**. List the standard sizes available and write a brief description of what they look like (e.g. colour, texture, sheen). Include any significant features they have, and any relevant information about how each is produced. After discussion, rate the strength and ease of use of the material on a scale of 1–5 (with 5 being the strongest or easiest to use).

MATERIAL	STANDARD SIZES	DESCRIPTION AND COMMENT (E.G. COLOUR, SOURCE, SUSTAINABILITY)	STRENGTH (1–5)	EASE OF USE (1–5)
Timber				
Radiata pine				
Dowel				
Plywood				
Other timbers				
Plastic				
Acrylic – sheet				
Other plastics				
Metal				
Threaded metal rod				
Flat metal bar				
Sheet metal				
Other metals				
Other materials				

WORKSHEET

NAME: DATE: / /

3.1 CLASSROOM SAFETY

1 Draw a map of your classroom (a bird's-eye view) in the space below. Make sure you include:

- tables or workbenches
- doors
- tools and equipment storage
- sinks
- spaces that you aren't allowed to enter without permission; e.g. machine rooms or storage areas (indicate these areas by shading them)
- any permanent machinery
- any safety features such as emergency stop buttons for the room, fire extinguishers, dust extractors, first aid cabinet, etc.

2 List **four** safety rules or guidelines for each of the four main areas of safety in the following table. (This can be completed in small groups and then shared with the rest of the class.)

Hand tools or equipment	Machinery
•	•
•	•
•	•
•	•

Movement (in and around the classroom)	Communication (speaking and listening)
•	•
•	•
•	•
•	•

3 To be safe in the classroom, what should you do if:

a you accidently break a tool?

b you need to use a tool or machine, but haven't been trained?

c you spill water on the floor?

d another student is using a tool in an incorrect or silly way, and might cause an injury?

4 The people in the images below are doing dangerous things. List the safety concerns or problems in each image.

3.2 TOOLS FOR TEXTILES, WOOD, METAL AND PLASTIC

1 Using the tools list on the right as a guide, name each tool in the table below. Choose different colours to fill in the highlight colours boxes. With the appropriate colour, Highlight each tool name according to whether it is a **marking**, **cutting**, **shaping**, **holding** or **joining** tool.

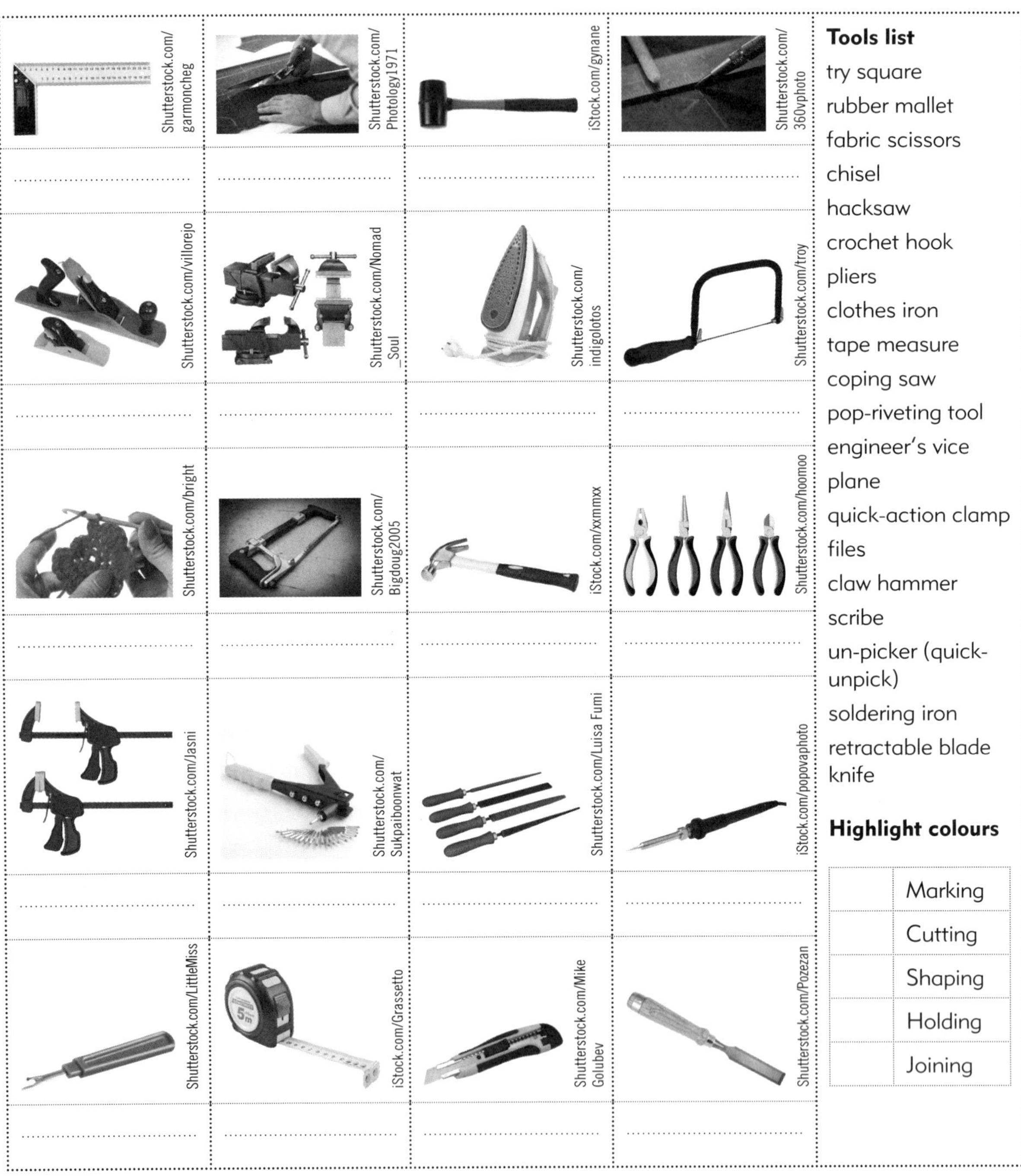

Tools list

try square
rubber mallet
fabric scissors
chisel
hacksaw
crochet hook
pliers
clothes iron
tape measure
coping saw
pop-riveting tool
engineer's vice
plane
quick-action clamp
files
claw hammer
scribe
un-picker (quick-unpick)
soldering iron
retractable blade knife

Highlight colours

	Marking
	Cutting
	Shaping
	Holding
	Joining

2 Describe **three** things you can do to look after the tools in your classroom to make sure they work properly and aren't damaged.

  9780170400206

JOINING

3 a If you needed to join two pieces of timber or metal together without using glue or welding, what fastenings could you use?

....

b What tools would you need to attach those fastenings?

....

4 What glues are suitable for joining the following materials?

a timber to timber: ....

b metal to timber: ....

c acrylic to acrylic: ....

d plastic to timber: ....

5 In the following table, describe what each of these machines do and the materials they can be used on.

Machine		Shutterstock.com/Sergio Stakhnyk	Shutterstock.com/topae	Shutterstock.com/Photoexpert
Name				
What does it do?				
Materials				

WORKSHEET

3.3 TOOLS CROSSWORD

CLUES

ACROSS

1 Cuts very thin sheet metal (3, 5)
5 Used to join wire and electrical components together (9, 4)
8 A machine used to cut wiggly lines and curves in thin material (5, 3)
11 A holding tool attached to your workbench (4)
12 Straight and strong; for measuring and marking (5, 4)
13 When making a rebate join, you need to use glue and ______ (5)
14 A battery-powered drilling tool (8, 5)
16 Measures curved shapes (8)
18 A power tool for making timber smooth (8, 6)
20 Turns and puts pressure on screws (11)
21 This portable machine cuts curves in timber (6)
23 Place this in a hole, squeeze the tool, and thin materials are joined (3, 5)
24 You must wear these when using a machine (6)

DOWN

2 Removes creases in fabric (5, 4)
3 Sharp and pointy; they hold fabric together (4)
4 A tool for removing wood to form a hollowed shape (5)
6 A circular tool used to hold fabric steady while decorative stitches are sewn (10, 4)
7 Cuts large pieces of wood along the grain (3, 3)
9 Jewellers use this to hold their work steady (1, 5)
10 Used for hand-sewing stitches through fabric (6)
15 Marks a point or position in metal or timber (6, 5)
17 A power tool that scratches lines and patterns into hard materials (8)
18 Cuts very fine, curvy lines in thin materials (8, 3)
19 Looks like a letter of the alphabet; a tool that holds materials steady (1, 5)
22 Used to tighten nuts and bolts (7)

  9780170400206

WORKSHEET

3.4 TRIALLING TECHNIQUES OR PROCESSES

Sometimes it's helpful to try different techniques or processes before making your product, so that you can:

- practise and increase your skills
- test the process to check it is suitable for the product in terms of function (e.g. is it strong enough?)
- see which technique or process looks good and suits your design.

TRIALLING

There are many online tutorials that can give you clear information about how to complete your techniques or processes.

Trialling is useful research for:

- joining processes
- finishing processes
- decorative techniques.

1 Choose three different techniques or processes that can be used for the same purpose.

a What type of techniques or processes are you trialling? ....

....

b Where are you going to use this on your product, or at what stage? ....

....

c Complete each of the following tables for your trials.

TRIAL 1

Where did you find instructions about how to complete this process?	
Draw or attach a photo of your finished trial.	How hard/easy was it to complete? What new things did you learn?
	Is this the best technique or process to use – why/why not?

TRIAL 2

Where did you find instructions about how to complete this process?	
Draw or attach a photo of your finished trial.	How hard/easy was it to complete? What new things did you learn?
	Is this the best technique or process to use – why/ why not?

TRIAL 3

Where did you find instructions about how to complete this process?	
Draw or attach a photo of your finished trial.	How hard/easy was it to complete? What new things did you learn?
	Is this the best technique or process to use – why/ why not?

9780170400206

WORKSHEET

3.5 MACHINE SAFETY

MACHINE SAFE-OPERATING PROCEDURES

Complete the following safe-operating procedure and competency check for a portable or permanent machine you may be using in class (not a sewing machine). This will require you to:

- draw or attach a picture of the machine and label its parts
- list the safety steps you need to follow before, during, and after using the machine
- Identify the correct Personal Protective Equipment (PPE) to wear (on the next page)
- record the date when you passed your safety test for each machine, and have your teacher sign your book.

<table>
<tr><td>NAME OF MACHINE:</td><td rowspan="2">SAFE-OPERATING PROCEDURES:
Setting up the machine and your work:

Connecting and safely using the machine:

After use, cleaning and packing up:</td></tr>
<tr><td>LABELLED ILLUSTRATION:</td></tr>
<tr><td>Personal Protective Equipment needed:</td><td>I passed my safety and competency test on:

TEACHER'S SIGNATURE:</td></tr>
</table>

NAME OF MACHINE:							
Required Personal Protective Equipment (PPE): (✓)							
Gloves	Face mask	Eye protection	Welding mask	Appropriate footwear	Hearing protection	Protective clothing	Face shield
☐	☐	☐	☐	☐	☐	☐	☐

Insert photo or drawing with labels:

Possible hazards:

Safe work procedure checklist:

1. Setting up the machine and your work:
   -
   -
   -
   -
2. Correct and safe use of the machine:
   -
   -
   -
   -
3. After use, cleaning and packing up:
   -
   -

The date I passed my competency test:

Teacher's signature:

 9780170400206

WORKSHEET

3.6 SEWING MACHINE LICENCE

NAME: DATE: / /

1 Name the parts of the sewing machine below or refer to a photo of one you are using. Use the words provided in the word bank to help you.

word bank

reverse control	bobbin winder	tension control	foot pedal
bobbin case compartment	stitch length adjustment	hand wheel	needle
spool pin/thread holder	thread take-up lever	light	stitch selector
stitch width adjustment	presser foot lever	presser foot	thread guide
fabric feed teeth	buttonhole control	drop feed control	
bobbin winder release			

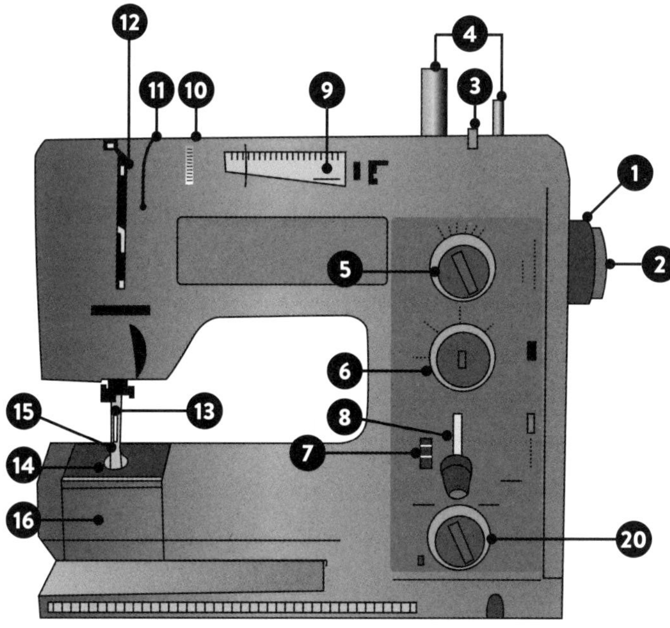

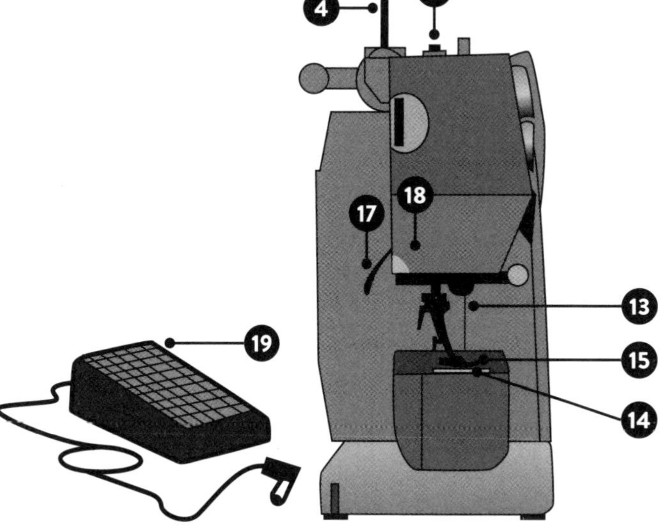

1

2

3

4

5

6

7

8

9

10

11

12

13

14

15

16

17

18

19

20

/10 MARKS

2 On the diagram, draw the path the thread would take when it is correctly threaded. /2 MARKS

3 When a bobbin is placed in the sewing machine, should the thread be in a clockwise or anti-clockwise direction?

.... /1 MARK

4 Why do you need to check the electrical cords when you are setting up the machine?

.... /1 MARK

5 Explain **two** other safety guidelines you need to follow when using a sewing machine.

....

.... /2 MARKS

6 Why should you never sew over a pin?

....

.... /1 MARKS

7 Describe **two** things that could go wrong if you don't pay attention while sewing.

....

.... /2 MARKS

8 What should you do with the machine when you have finished sewing?

.... /1 MARK

TOTAL SCORE /20 MARKS

PASS	NEED TO RE-SIT TEST

WORKSHEET

3.7 SEWING MACHINE PRACTICE

HOW ACCURATELY CAN YOU SEW?

Trace the following design onto heavy tracing paper or baking paper. Carefully sew over the lines (with or without thread). For some of the lines, you will need to set your machine to a zigzag stitch – don't try to match up the points. The best place to start is probably the outside lines of the design with the straight and curvy lines. How well can you follow the lines?

WORKSHEET

3.8 JOINING METHODS

1 Name each of the **timber** joints shown, and explain where they might be used in a product.

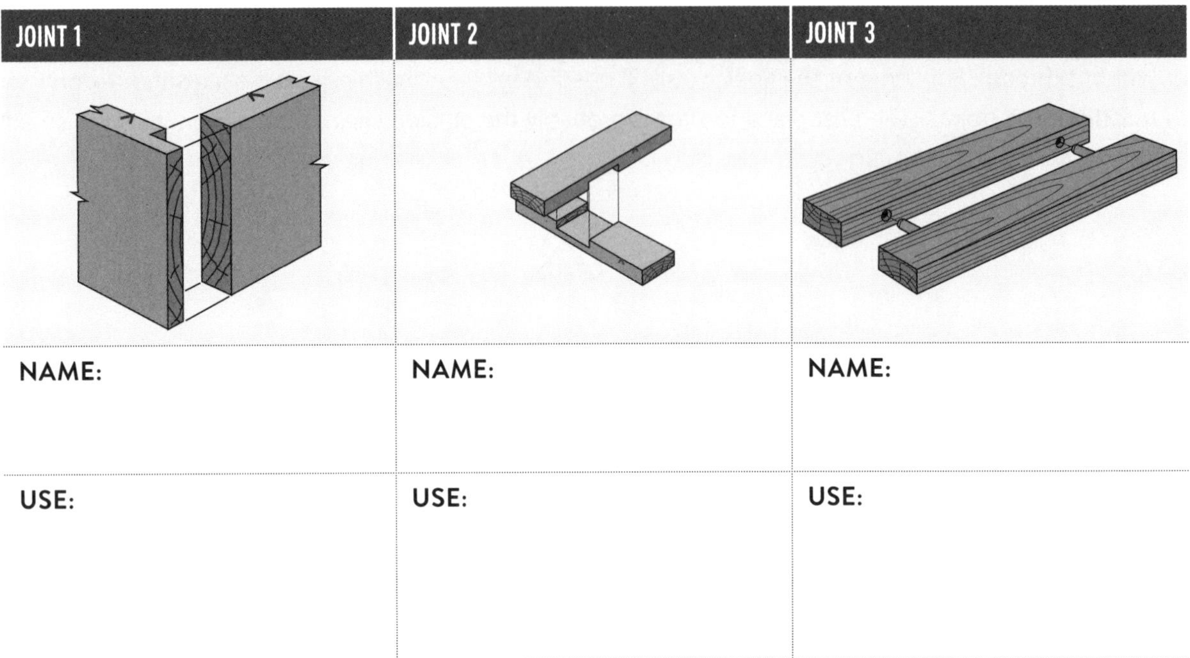

JOINT 1	JOINT 2	JOINT 3
NAME:	NAME:	NAME:
USE:	USE:	USE:

2 Name each of the **metal** joins shown, and explain where they might be used in a product.

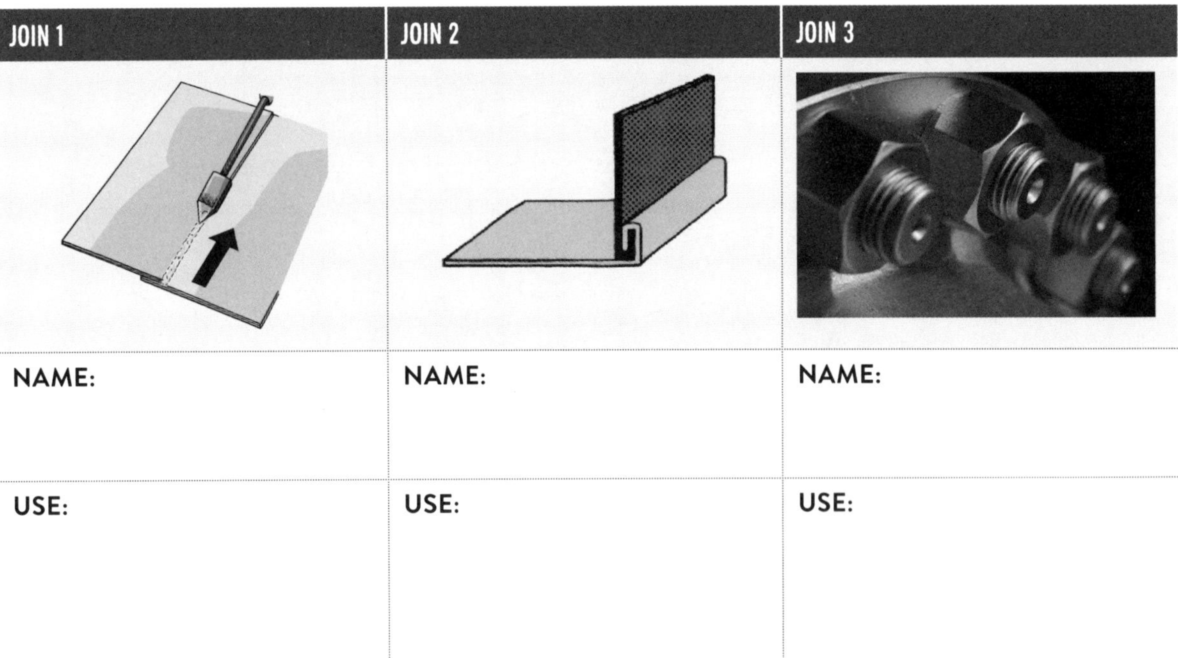

JOIN 1	JOIN 2	JOIN 3
NAME:	NAME:	NAME:
USE:	USE:	USE:

3 Name each of the **textiles** joins/seams shown, and explain where they might be used in a product.

JOIN 1	JOIN 2	JOIN 3
	Wrong side	
NAME:	NAME:	NAME:
USE:	USE:	USE:

4 a Choose one of the joins from question 1, 2 or 3, and explain with step-by-step instructions how to make it.

Join: ....

Instructions: ....

....

....

....

b List the tools needed to make the join.

....

c Describe two safety rules you need to follow while making the join.

....

....

5 What are the general names of the following fasteners, and which materials are they used to join?

Fastener:	iStock.com/qhrome27	iStock.com/EuToch	Shutterstock.com/ Jame Pakpoom	Shutterstock.com/Jomic
Name:				
Materials:				

WORKSHEET

3.9 JOINING METHODS – RESEARCH ACTIVITY

1 Find examples of **three** different joining methods that could be used for your product. For each join, find out the information required to complete the tables below. (For disadvantages, think about strength and durability, skills required, time, specialised tools, etc.)

Joining method 1 (diagram or picture)	Name: ....
	Where could it be used in your product? ....
	What tools are required? ....
	What are the disadvantages or problems with this method? ....

Joining method 2 (diagram or picture)	Name: ....
	Where could it be used in your product? ....
	What tools are required? ....
	What are the disadvantages or problems with this method? ....

Joining method 3 (diagram or picture)	Name:
	Where could it be used in your product?
	What tools are required?
	What are the disadvantages or problems with this method?

CONCLUSIONS

2 Choose the joining method that would be the best to use for your product and explain your choice in the space below.

METHOD	REASON FOR CHOICE

3 What new skills would you need to practise to be able to use this joining method well?

WORKSHEET

3.10 DECORATIVE TECHNIQUES

1 Choose **one** of the decorative techniques for your material of choice (some ideas can be found in the *Tech by Design Student Book* on pages 85–87, 100, 106–107, and 110–111). Research where the decorative technique came from and how it is carried out. Using this information, complete the following table.

Draw or attach a photo of the decorative technique	
Is this a traditional or cultural decorative technique? From where does it originate? …………………… ……………………	What do you like about this technique? …………………… ……………………
Does it use a new form of technology? …………………… ……………………	How is this technique completed? What special tools are required? …………………… …………………… …………………… …………………… …………………… …………………… …………………… ……………………
On what types of material can it be used? …………………… ……………………	
In what different ways can it be used on a product? …………………… ……………………	

2 Some newer technologies that can be used to create decorative forms and patterns are listed in the word bank below.

word bank

laser cutter and engraver | 3D printer | digital printer | vacuum former

Choose **two** of these technologies and complete the following table to explain what they can be used to create. (If you know of other forms of technology, you can explain these instead.)

TECHNOLOGY	WHAT CAN IT DO (DECORATIVELY)?	WHAT MATERIALS IS IT SUITABLE FOR?

WORKSHEET

NAME: DATE: / /

4.1 FORCES

It is important to understand the forces acting around us. A force is a push or a pull applied to an object.

REMEMBER The five main forces are:

- compression – a squashing force
- tension – a stretching force
- shear – two forces pushing inwards but past each other, causing a cutting effect
- torsion – a twisting force
- refraction – a bending force.

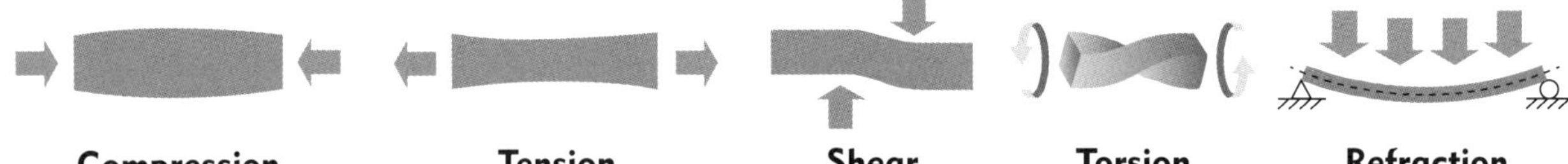

1 For each of the force images below, name the main force applied.

FORCE IMAGE	FORCE TYPE
Cutting hair Shutterstock.com/Voyagerix	What type of force is applied to the hair?
Vice gripping an egg Shutterstock.com/By Bildagentur Zoonar GmbH	What type of force is applied to the egg?
Bending a weight bar Getty Images/John Wilhelm is a photoholic	Which force is the child applying to the weight bar?
Stretching chewing gum <source line to come>	Which force is the child applying to the chewing gum?
Wringing out a towel iStock.com/Sasilstock	Which force are the hands applying to the towel?

WORKSHEET

4.2 LEVERS

REMEMBER

Levers come in three different classes depending on which order the effort (E), load (L) and fulcrum (F) are arranged.

- Class 1 levers – the fulcrum is between the effort and load, which move in opposite directions.
- Class 2 levers – the load is between the effort and fulcrum, and load and effort move in the same direction.
- Class 3 levers – the effort is between the fulcrum and load, and the load moves in the same direction as the effort.

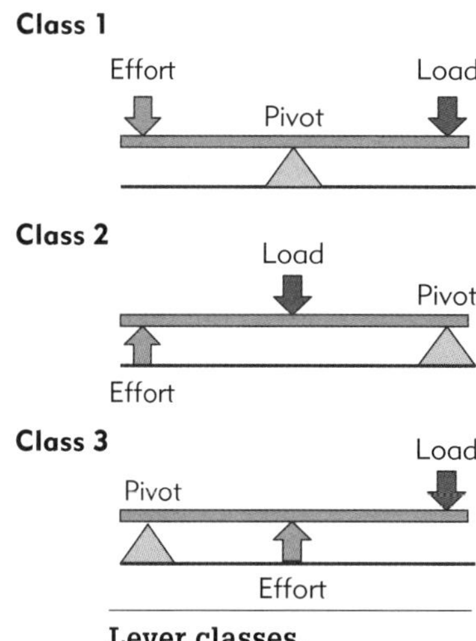

Lever classes.

Lever classes can be remembered by the mnemonic:
EFL ELF FEL

MECHANICAL ADVANTAGE

REMEMBER

- Speed advantage – when the effort is closer to the fulcrum than the load is to the fulcrum.
- Force advantage – when the load is closer to the fulcrum than the effort is to the fulcrum.
- No advantage – when the load and the effort are the same distance from the fulcrum.

Effort = input; load = output; fulcrum = pivot.

1 For each image in the following table:

a label the effort, load and fulcrum

b describe the lever class by referring to the diagrams at top right

c state whether the lever gives a force advantage, speed advantage or no advantage.

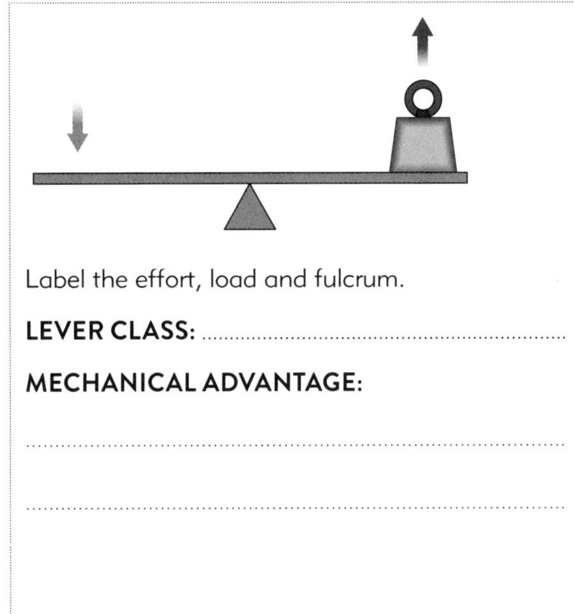 Label the effort, load and fulcrum. **LEVER CLASS:** .... **MECHANICAL ADVANTAGE:**	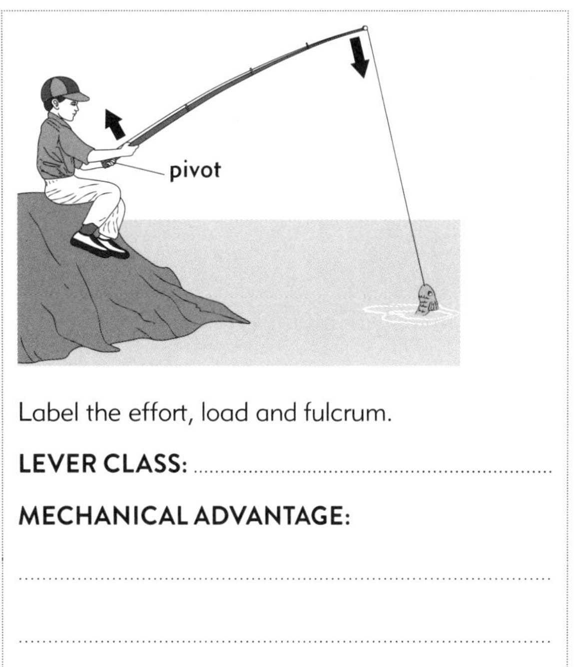 Label the effort, load and fulcrum. **LEVER CLASS:** .... **MECHANICAL ADVANTAGE:** ....

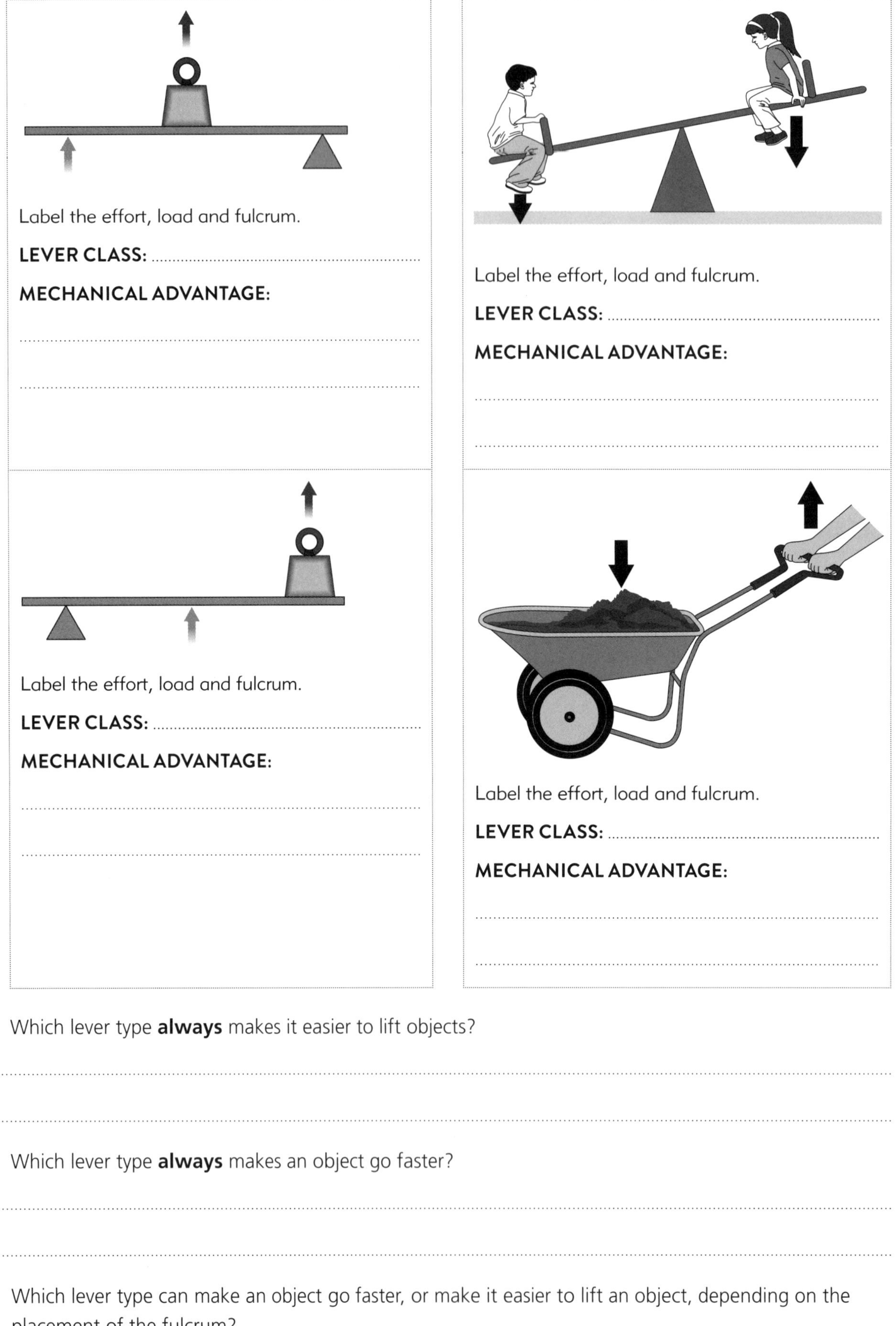

2 Which lever type **always** makes it easier to lift objects?

....

....

3 Which lever type **always** makes an object go faster?

....

....

4 Which lever type can make an object go faster, or make it easier to lift an object, depending on the placement of the fulcrum?

....

....

WORKSHEET

4.3 SIMPLE MACHINES

Image 1 Lever allowing user to lift a load

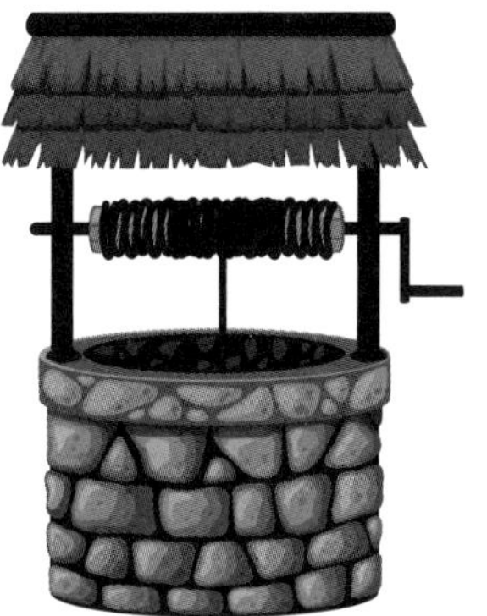

Image 2 Crank handle turning drum

Image 3 Pulley allowing user to lift a load

Three simple machines making it easier to move a load

REMEMBER

The four motions that are utilised by machines are:

- linear motion – an object moving in a straight line
- rotary motion – an object moving in a circle or part of a circle (an arc)
- reciprocal motion – backward and forward motion in a straight line
- oscillating motion – backward and forward motion in an arc.

The image at right of a crank driving a piston is an example of rotary motion being transformed into reciprocal motion.

Input = rotary motion of crank

Output = reciprocal motion of piston

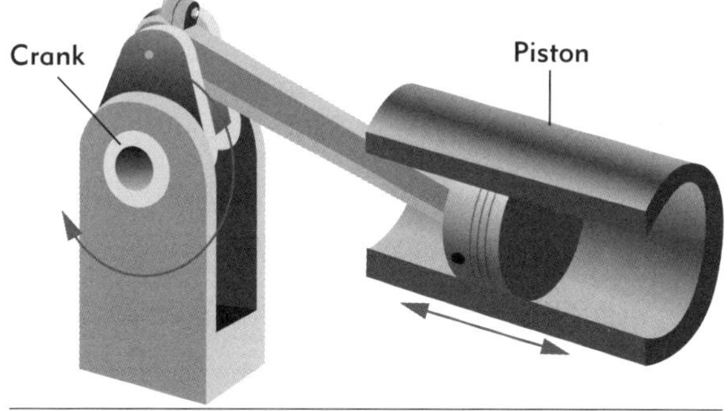

A crank driving a piston

1 a Describe the type of input motion of the lever pictured at the top of the page (top left)

....

....

b Describe the output motion of the same lever as in Question 1a.

....

....

c What are the differences between the input and output motions of the lever?

....

....

2 a Describe the type of input motion of the crank turning a drum, as pictured at the top of the page (top middle)

....

....

b Describe the type of output motion of the crank.

c What are the differences between the type of input and output motions of a crank?

3 a Describe the type of input motion of a pulley, as pictured on the previous page (top right).

b Describe the type of output motion of a pulley.

c What are the differences between the type of input and output motions of a pulley?

4 a Name another simple machine.

b Describe the type of input motion for the machine.

c Describe the type of output motion for the machine.

d What are the differences between the input and output motions of the machine?

WORKSHEET

4.4 COMBINING MACHINES

1 a Describe the function of all of the simple machines combined.

....

....

b Using the following word bank, label as many simple machines as possible in the boat winch shown.

word bank

spur gear	worm gear	rack	idler	worm wheel
crank handle	cam	follower	pulley system	crank
drum	lever	wedge		

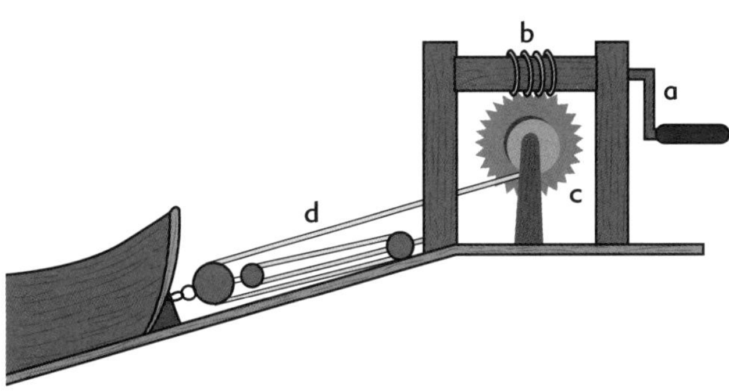

2 In the table below, name and describe the purpose for each of the simple machines labeled above. Some answers are provided.

NAME	PURPOSE
a Crank handle	
b	
c	
d	Creates a force advantage

9780170400206

WORKSHEET

4.5 ELECTRICITY

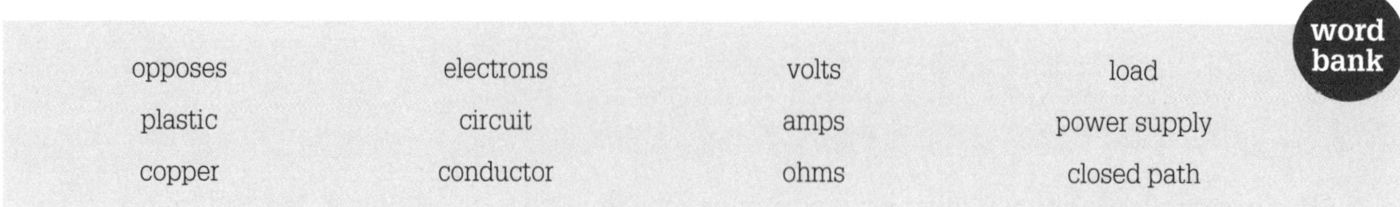

1 Using the word bank above, complete the definitions of the following important electrical terms:

a **Conductor** – All circuits require a conductor for the electricity to flow through. Conductors are usually made from .... because it has low electrical resistance.

b **Insulator** – Wires are often wrapped in .... to stop the electricity leaving the wire. High-voltage wires are always insulated to keep you safe. An insulator stops or hinders the flow of electricity.

c **Resistance** – Resistance is the force that .... the current in a circuit. Every component has some resistance. The symbol for resistance is Ω (the Greek letter omega).

d **Current** – Current is the flow of .... in a circuit. Current is measured in amperes or amps. In electronics, we use very small currents. A light-emitting diode (LED) typically uses 7 milliamps (which is seven-thousandths of one amp).

e **Voltage** – Voltage is the force that pushes electrons around a .... The unit to measure voltage is volts.

2 a What are the three parts that all circuits must contain?

....

b What makes a circuit work (i.e. gives it power)?

....

3 Both of the following drawings are of a torch.

a Which of these diagrams is a circuit diagram? (circle the correct one)

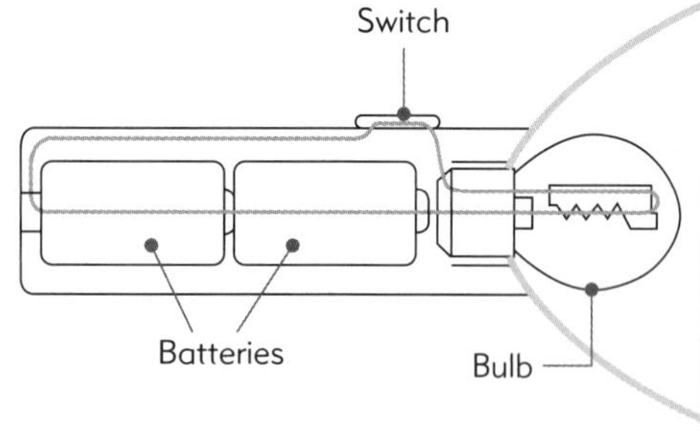

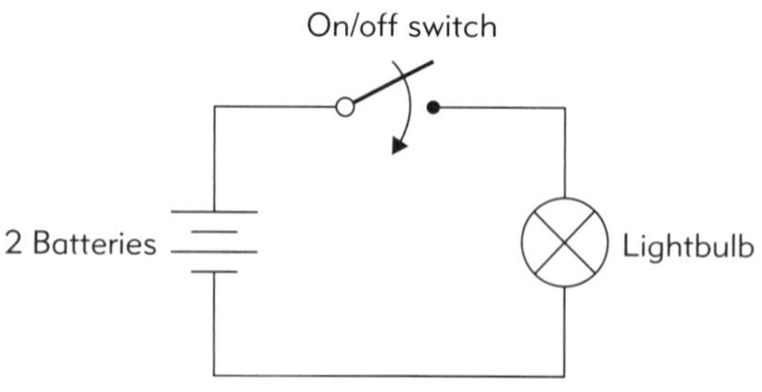

4 Why do we draw circuit diagrams like this? Why do we use symbols to represent different parts of a circuit?

....

....

WORKSHEET

4.6 COMPONENTS

word bank

LED	resistor	switch	lamp
transistor	capacitor	diode	battery/cell
motor			

1 Use the terms in the word bank above to answer the following questions.

a Name the electrical components shown below.

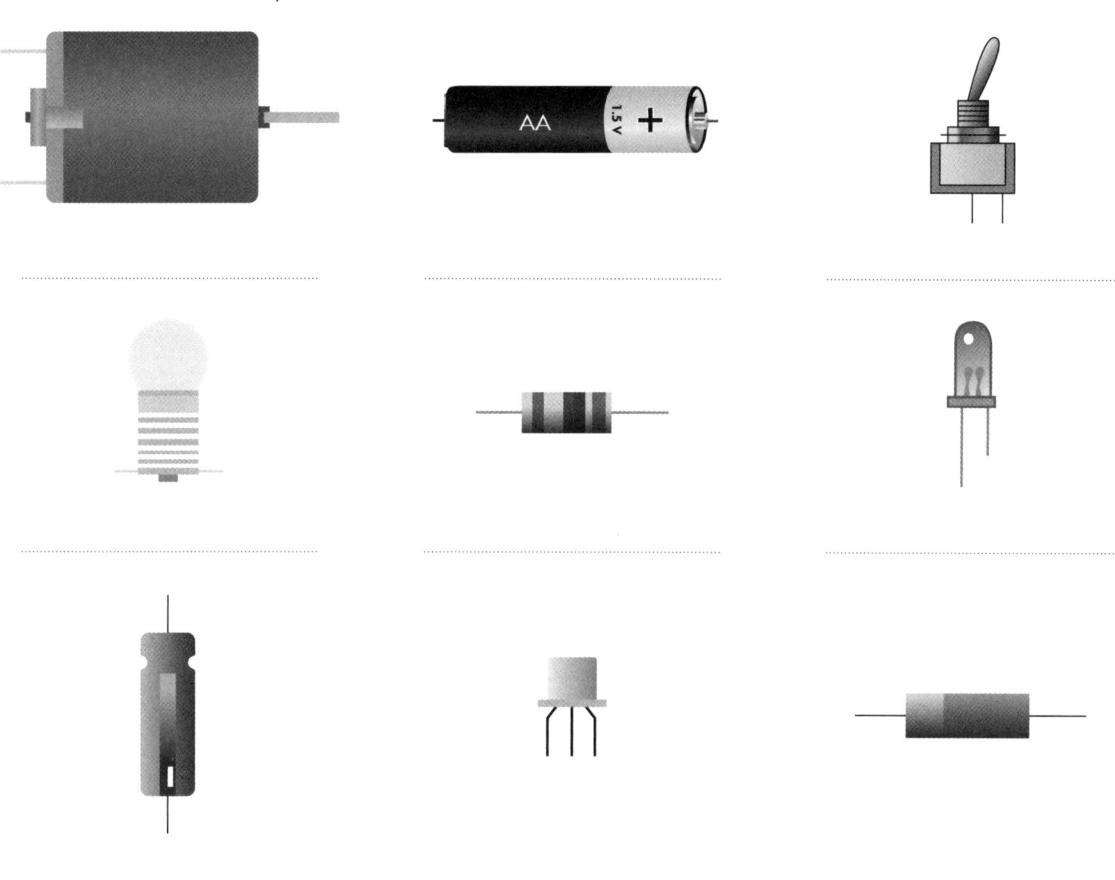

b Name the following symbols that identify electrical components in a circuit diagram.

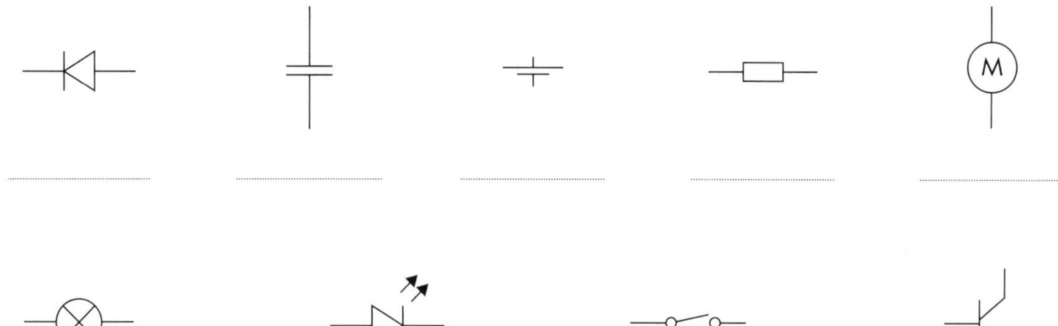

WORKSHEET

4.7 DRAWING CIRCUITS

Use the circuit diagrams with symbols to draw illustrations of what the circuits might look like in real life. This activity will be easier if you first complete Worksheet 4.6. Use the first entry as an example.

CIRCUIT SYMBOLS	REAL-LIFE CIRCUIT
Example: switched motor circuit diagram 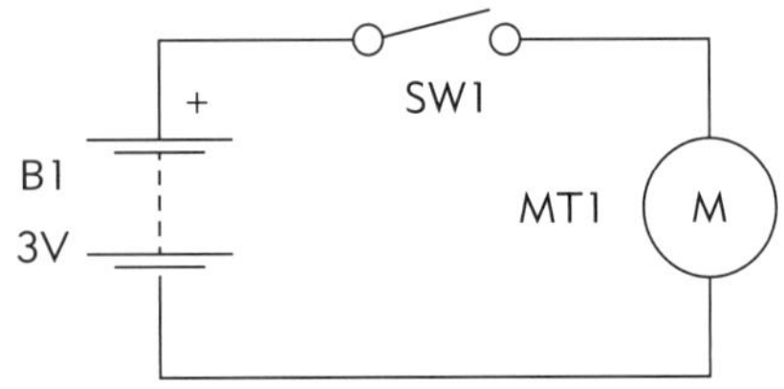 B1 3V, SW1, MT1 M	Example: switched motor circuit real-life illustration 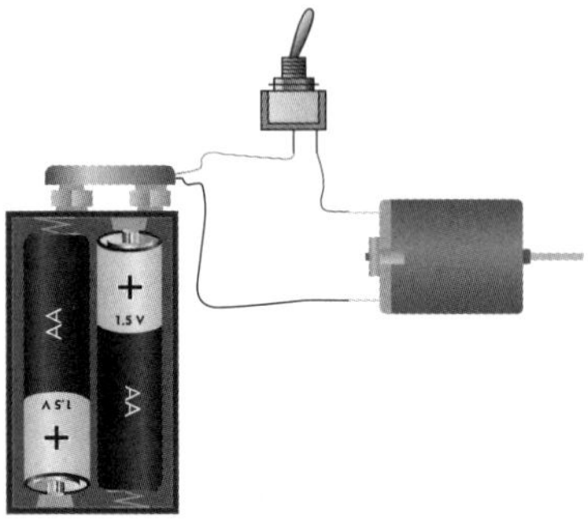 AA 1.5 V, AA 1.5 V
Lamp circuit 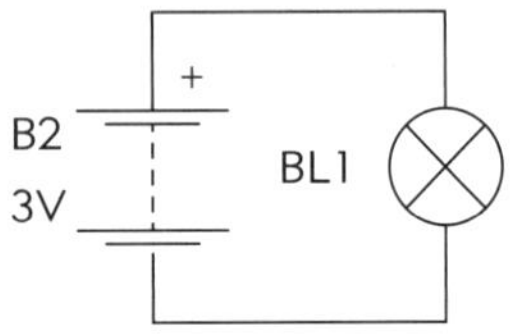 B2 3V, BL1	
Series lamp circuit 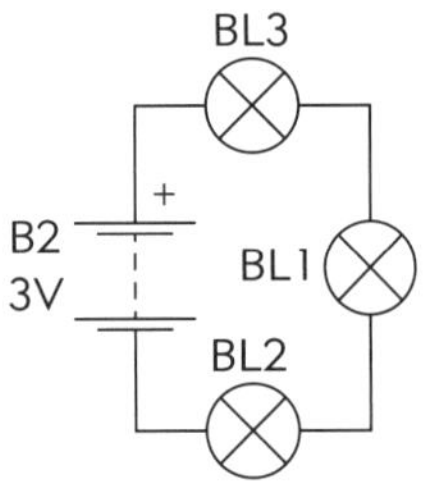 BL3, B2 3V, BL1, BL2	
LED circuit 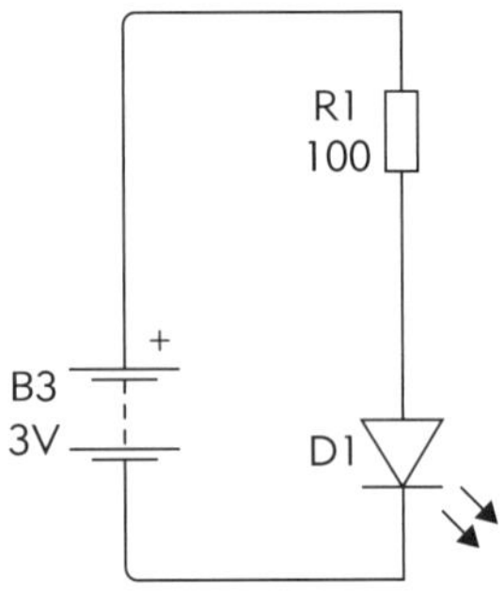 R1 100, B3 3V, D1	
Toggle switch motor circuit 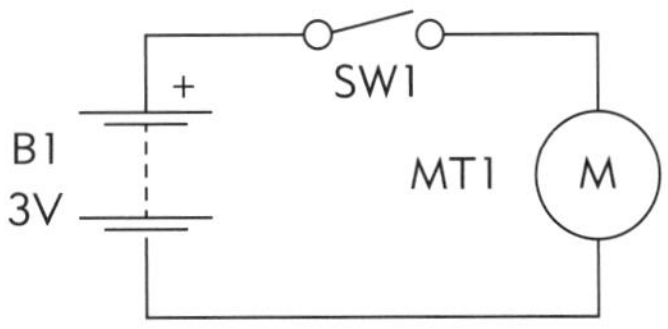 SW1, B1 3V, MT1 M	

WORKSHEET

4.8 RESISTOR COLOUR CODES

REMEMBER Resistor values are shown by colour codes. Normally there are four coloured bands, but sometimes five are used.

With a four-band resistor, the first two bands represent the digits 0–9. The third band represents the number of zeros, and the fourth band shows the tolerance (how accurate the resistor is, as a percentage).

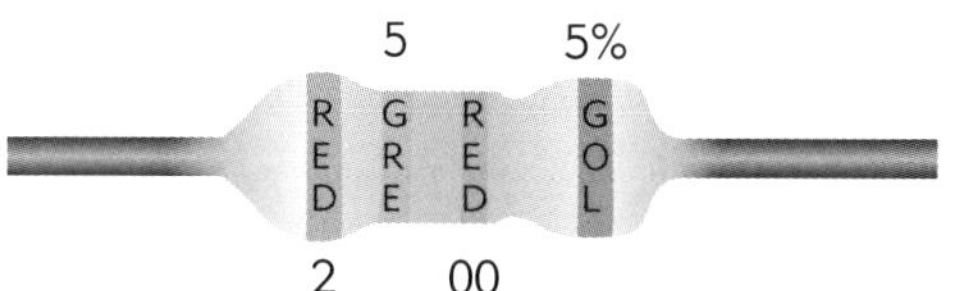

Resistors have the first three bands placed together, with a slightly larger gap before the fourth band. This resistor has a value of 2500 ohms with 5% tolerance.

COLOUR	FIRST BAND	SECOND BAND	THIRD BAND	FOURTH BAND TOLERANCE
Black (BLA)	0	0	–	–
Brown (BRO)	1	1	0	1 %
Red (RED)	2	2	00	2%
Orange (ORA)	3	3	000	–
Yellow (YEL)	4	4	0000	–
Green (GRE)	5	5	00000	–
Blue (BLU)	6	6	000000	–
Violet (VIO)	7	7	–	–
Grey (GRY)	8	8	–	–
White (WHI)	9	9	–	–
Gold (GOL)	–	–	–	5%
Silver (SIL)	–	–	–	10%

DETERMINING THE VALUE OF RESISTORS

1 Use the table above to calculate the value of the following resistors. Show your working in the space provided.

a Brown, red, yellow, silver

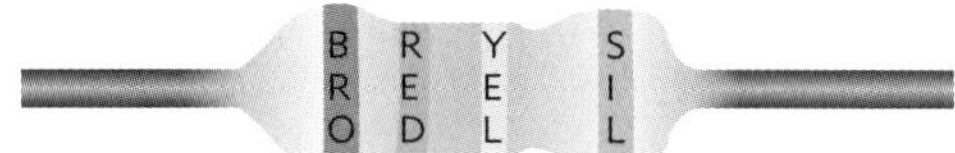

Resistor value:

b Orange, white, brown, gold

Resistor value:

c Orange, white, black, brown

Resistor value:

DRAWING RESISTORS

2 Use the table on the previous page to determine the bands for resistors with the following values. Colour and identify the first three blank bands provided.

a Resistor value: 22 000 Ω

b Resistor value: 470 Ω

WORKSHEET

4.9 INPUT–PROCESS–OUTPUT AND CONTROL

1 We often think of electrical systems in terms of **input**, **process**, **control** and **output**. Define the following terms:

a input

....

b process

....

c control

....

d output

....

2 Identify one of the main inputs, processes, controls and outputs for the following electrical systems or products.

PRODUCT	INPUT	PROCESS	CONTROL	OUTPUT
Toaster				
Torch				
House alarm				
Air conditioner				

3 Some products have a number of inputs and outputs. In the following table, think about and discuss a **mobile phone**. What are its many inputs and outputs? How is a mobile phone controlled?

PRODUCT	INPUT	PROCESS	CONTROL	OUTPUT
Mobile phone		*Complicated integrated circuits and microcomputer systems*		

CHALLENGE 5.1

STORE-IT DESIGN CHALLENGE

DESIGN CHALLENGE 5.1: STORE-IT

Design and produce a shelf or container that holds items such as DVDs, game discs, jewellery, trophies, collections and phones/chargers.

REQUIREMENTS (LIMITS OR CONSTRAINTS)

- Your product should be no larger than the size set by your teacher.
- Choose from the joining methods specified by your teacher.
- Use the materials available in your school (or provide special materials from home).
- If you are designing and making a shelf, **no simple box shapes are allowed** – think of other shapes, or ways to use rectangles.
- Your design must have some **form of decoration** such as shapes, painting or metal scrolling.
- Use at least two different materials (such as wood, metal, plastics and/or fabric).
- Don't create too many divisions or make them too complex.

DESIGN CHOICES

You will need to make decisions regarding:

- the shape of your storage solution (within the size limits)
- materials you will use
- joins you will use to construct your design (within the teacher's set requirements)
- decorative design.

TASKS

To complete the Store-it challenge, you need to carry out a range of design tasks. These can be done using Template A on page 129 in Part Three of this workbook, and by referring to pages 140–144 of the *Tech by Design Student Book*.

Your work should include (use this as a checklist – tick as you complete each task):

- ☐ A mind map (or another type of graphic organiser) exploring aspects of storage.
- ☐ A design web and brief.
- ☐ Criteria for success – explaining what you expect in a good storage product.
- ☐ Research into materials, joining materials (page 63), existing products or the design situation.
- ☐ Design sketches and design options.
- ☐ A cutting list for the materials you need.
- ☐ A production plan that includes all the steps you need to carry out to make your storage product.
- ☐ A journal that records your production using photos and written reflections.
- ☐ An evaluation of your finished storage solution using your criteria for success as a starting point.

 9780170400206

RESEARCH – JOINING DIFFERENT MATERIALS

This design challenge asks you to use more than one type of material to make your storage solution. If you want your product to last, you need to know how to join different materials to each other effectively.

1 Investigate **three** ways to join different materials **physically**; e.g. using nuts and bolts, screws, rivets, threaded rod, eyelets, cut and interlocked materials.

Draw a diagram of each joining method

JOINING METHOD 1	JOINING METHOD 2	JOINING METHOD 3
Advantages:	Advantages:	Advantages:
Disadvantages:	Disadvantages:	Disadvantages:
Where could you use this method?	Where could you use this method?	Where could you use this method?
Tools and equipment:	Tools and equipment:	Tools and equipment:
Safety:	Safety:	Safety:

2 Investigate **two** different glues you could use to join **different** materials.

GLUING METHOD 1	GLUING METHOD 2
Name of glue:	Name of glue:
Materials it can join:	Materials it can join:
Working time:	Working time:
Drying time:	Drying time:
Safety requirements:	Safety requirements:
Advantages:	Advantages:
Disadvantages:	Disadvantages:
Tools and equipment:	Tools and equipment:

3 Which physical joining method is the strongest? ....

....

4 Which method looks the best? Why? ....

....

....

5 Which joining methods will suit your design ideas best? Why? ....

....

....

Use the General template (A) starting on page 129 to complete your challenge.

CARRY-IT DESIGN CHALLENGE

DESIGN CHALLENGE 5.2: CARRY-IT

Design and make a fabric carrier for holding and moving objects of your choice. The carrier can be designed and made for you, or for someone else. It should be comfortable to wear, and keep its content secure while being moved. You also need to think about the specific needs of person who will use the carrier.

REQUIREMENTS (LIMITS OR CONSTRAINTS)

- Your product should be no larger than the size set by your teacher.
- Use at least two different types of fabric, one of which needs to be **recycled**.
- Include a method of keeping the contents **secure** (such as a fastening or flap).
- Include a feature that will make it **comfortable** to wear or hold.
- Incorporate some **form of decoration** to make it individual and easily recognisable.
- Use at least two forms of stitching or joins.

DESIGN CHOICES

You will need to make decisions regarding:

- what your carrier will hold
- the form, shape and size of your carrier (within the limits set by your teacher)
- how it will work
- decorative design and techniques (a range of these will be shown to you by your teacher).

TASKS

To complete the Carry-it challenge, you need to carry out a range of design tasks. These can be done using Template A on page 129 in Part Three of this workbook, and by referring to pages 144–148 of the *Tech by Design Student Book*.

Your work should include (use this as a checklist – tick as you complete each task):

- [ ] The bag trial (page 66), or a mind map exploring aspects of carry bags/packs.
- [ ] A design web and brief explaining your need.
- [ ] Criteria for success – explaining what you expect in a good product.
- [ ] Research into sustainable materials (page 67), bag shapes, seams and joining methods or decorative techniques.
- [ ] Design sketches of your initial ideas and design options showing fully worked-out design concepts.
- [ ] A cutting list describing the materials you need to make your carry bag/pack.
- [ ] A production plan that describes all of the steps needed to make your product.
- [ ] A journal that records your production using photos and written reflections.
- [ ] An evaluation of your finished carrying solution using your criteria for success as a starting point.

TRIALLING DIFFERENT BAGS AND BACKPACKS

In small groups, find examples of three different bags or packs, and investigate and report on them using the following questions.

1 Take a photo and describe the following aspects of each bag.
   a How big is it?
   b What material is it made from?
   c What does it look like? (e.g. describe shapes, colours, contrast, texture, decoration/patterning)
   d How do you carry it?
   e What compartments and closures/ fastenings does it have?
   f Does it look like any of the bags were designed for a specific task?

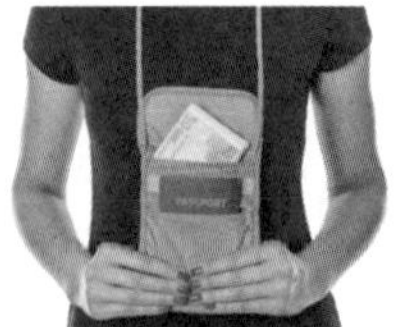

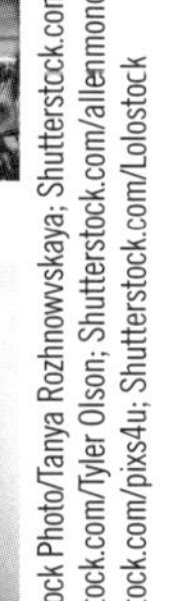

People use carrying solutions in many different situations.

Alamy Stock Photo/Tanya Rozhnowvskaya; Shutterstock.com/Saklakova; Shutterstock.com/Tyler Olson; Shutterstock.com/allenmondorphoto; Shutterstock.com/pixs4u; Shutterstock.com/Lolostock

2 Put a heavy load in each bag and carry it around the classroom. Record your observations as follows:
   a Is it easy to put the load in each bag?
   b How comfortable is each bag to carry when loaded?
   c Does it feel like the load is safely held (i.e. it won't easily fall out)?

3 Compare and analyse the bags by answering the following questions:
   a Which bag is the most comfortable? Why?
   b Which bag do you think is the strongest? Why?
   c Which bag do you think looks the best? Why?
   d Which bag suits its purpose most (i.e. is best at doing the job it is designed to do)?

RESEARCH: MATERIALS – HOW SUSTAINABLE ARE THEY?

1 Gather **three** examples of fabrics that could be used to make a carry bag (find examples that are made from different fibres). Fill in the tables below with information you have found about these fibres. Information about sustainability issues related to fibres can be found in the *Tech by Design* Student Book (pages 53–57) or the Eco Design Textiles QuickGuide on the DATTA Vic website (sustainability resources page).

	SAMPLE 1 – FIBRE: ______	SAMPLE 2 – FIBRE: ______	SAMPLE 3 – FIBRE: ______
Sample piece (attach a small sample of the fabric in the space provided)			
Where was this fabric made? How far has it travelled to get to you?			
Sustainability – find out any issues related to the sourcing of this fibre (good or bad)			

2 Could any of these fabrics be replaced by recycled fabrics? ....

....

3 What sort of fabric clothing or product would work well when recycled? ....

....

4 Where could you source these types of recycled items? ....

....

5 Why is recycling fabric a good sustainability strategy? ....

....

6 What does the term 'up-cycling' mean? ....

....

....

Use the General template (A) starting on page 129 to complete your challenge.

CHALLENGE 5.3

SHOW-IT DESIGN CHALLENGE

DESIGN CHALLENGE 5.3: SHOW-IT

Design and make a display solution for holding, protecting and displaying a favourite photo. This product could be for your use, or for your family or friends.

REQUIREMENTS (LIMITS OR CONSTRAINTS)

- Your product needs to hold a standard sized photo (either 7.5 cm × 12.5 cm, or 10 cm × 15 cm).
- The photo needs to be **easy to see**.
- The photo needs to be **protected**.
- You must be able to **change the photo easily**.
- The display product needs to be able to **stand on a flat surface**.
- Include at least two different materials in your design.

DESIGN CHOICES

You will need to make decisions regarding:

- the shape and size of your display solution, and what size of photo it will be made for
- how you will include materials and colour
- the stand method/structure you will use
- the method used for holding and changing photos.
- a decorative feature (may match a photo)

DESIGN CHALLENGE TASKS

To complete the Show-it challenge, you need to carry out a range of design tasks. These can be done using Template A on page 129 in Part Three of this workbook, and by referring to pages 148–151 of the *Tech by Design Student Book*.

Your work should include (use this as a checklist – tick as you complete each task):

- ☐ Research into sheet acrylic (page 69).
- ☐ A design web and brief that explains who you are making the display for and what it will hold.
- ☐ Criteria for success – explaining what you expect in a good display product.
- ☐ Design sketches and design options – using the template pages to explore different ideas, and then developing well-thought-out options.
- ☐ A cutting list to identify all of the materials you will need (don't forget that you need to include two different sorts of materials).
- ☐ A production plan that includes the steps you need to carry out to make your photo display, and safety guidelines for each step.
- ☐ A journal that uses photos and words to record your experiences while making your product.
- ☐ An evaluation of your finished display solution using your criteria for success as a starting point.

ACRYLIC FACTS AND FUN

1 What is the scientific name for sheet acrylic? ....

2 What other common names are used for acrylic? ....

....

3 a What do the terms 'thermoset' and 'thermoplastic' mean when referring to plastics? ....

....

....

b Is acrylic a 'thermoset' or 'thermoplastic' plastic? ....

4 How is sheet acrylic made? ....

....

5 List **four** products that are commonly made from sheet acrylic.

....

....

6 What temperature should you set an oven to when heating sheet acrylic? ....

....

7 What does the term 'plastic memory' mean? ....

....

8 Which acrylic bending or forming methods might be useful in your Show-it design? Explain how you might use these methods.

....

....

9 How sustainable is acrylic sheet? Can it be recycled? How can you reduce waste?

....

....

THE FUN BIT!

Trial different ways of bending and forming acrylic, such as:

- heating a thin strip of acrylic in an oven and then twisting
- using a strip heater to fold acrylic
- pressing solid shapes into heated acrylic
- heating and slumping acrylic into a shape/form.

Use the General template (A) starting on page 129 to complete your challenge.

CHALLENGE 5.4

MINI STORAGE DESIGN CHALLENGE

DESIGN CHALLENGE 5.4: MINI STORAGE

Design and make a casing for a USB flash drive that is individual and easy to recognise.

REQUIREMENTS (LIMITS OR CONSTRAINTS)

- Your product needs to **stand out** and have features that make it **easily recognisable**.
- The casing must **fit tightly** onto the USB flash drive's inner component.
- Your product must be **comfortable** to hold and easy to grab when inserting and removing the USB flash drive's from a device.

Shutterstock.com/Coprid

A USB flash drive (left) could be covered by this student design (right)

- Use materials available in your school (this might include sheet plastic, 3D printing plastic or bamboo plywood).

DESIGN CHOICES

You will need to make design decisions regarding:

- the shape and colour of the casing
- whether your design will be abstract (based on simple shapes and patterns), or have recognisable features (based on letters or an object)
- the materials you will use.
- how it will be constructed

TASKS

To complete the Mini Storage challenge, you need to carry out a range of design tasks. These can be done using Template A on page 129 in Part Three of this workbook, and by referring to pages 151–154 of the *Tech by Design Student Book*.

Your work should include (use this as a checklist – tick as you complete each task):

- [ ] Research into sheet materials, (Questions 5 and 6 of Worksheet 2.3, page 24) or 3D printing materials (page 71) and using CAD (page 71).
- [ ] A design web and brief to explore and define possibilities for design.
- [ ] Criteria for success – explaining what you expect in a good mini-storage product.
- [ ] Design sketches and design options – your finished design options can be done using CAD software on an app (page 71).
- [ ] A cutting list if you are making your USB holder from sheet material.
- [ ] A production plan that describes the steps you need to follow to make you USB holder.
- [ ] A journal that records your production using photos and written reflections.
- [ ] An evaluation of your finished mini-storage solution using your criteria for success as a starting point.

RESEARCH: MATERIALS FOR 3D PRINTING

1 The two main materials used in 3D printers are ABS and PLA. What do these initials stand for?

....

....

2 What are these filaments made from or how are they sourced?

....

....

3 a What are the environmental/sustainability issues related to each of these materials?

....

....

b Which do you think might be a more sustainable choice? Why?

....

....

4 What are the physical differences between the two materials? (e.g. colour range, sheen, melt temperature)

....

....

USING CAD

CAD stands for computer-aided drawing. There are different types of CAD software, and apps, that can be used to develop designs – these design files are used to 'drive' 3D printers. It is important to become familiar with the particular software or app you will use for designing your mini-storage casing. Your teacher will explain some of the basics, but to help you explore what you can do, try the following tasks.

1 Draw some simple, solid 3D forms (e.g. cube, sphere, cone).

2 Repeat one of these shapes a number of times and resize so each one is different. How do you know how big your objects are?

3 Cut holes of different sizes and shapes into some of your forms, some part of the way through and others right through.

4 Put some of these shapes together (from tasks 1–3 above) to create an interesting geometric form.

5 Put shapes together to create a simple animal shape.

6 Learn how to save your design in the right file format for 3D printing (usually .stl files).

Use the General template (A) starting on page 129 to complete your challenge.

CHALLENGE 6.1

CRANK AND CAM AUTOMATON DESIGN CHALLENGE

DESIGN CHALLENGE 6.1: CRANK AND CAM AUTOMATON

Design and make an automaton with a moving part (such as a child fishing with a fishing rod that moves up and down as a fish is caught, a cat jumping, or a runner's leg moving up and down). There must be minimal friction to operate smoothly and effectively and your product must be well-finished to look its best.

REQUIREMENTS (LIMITS OR CONSTRAINTS)

- The product size will be set by your teacher.
- Use the materials available in your school (or provide special materials from home).
- Your design must have a moving part.
- The object must be moved by a cam and pushrod.
- Your automaton must be powered by a crank handle.

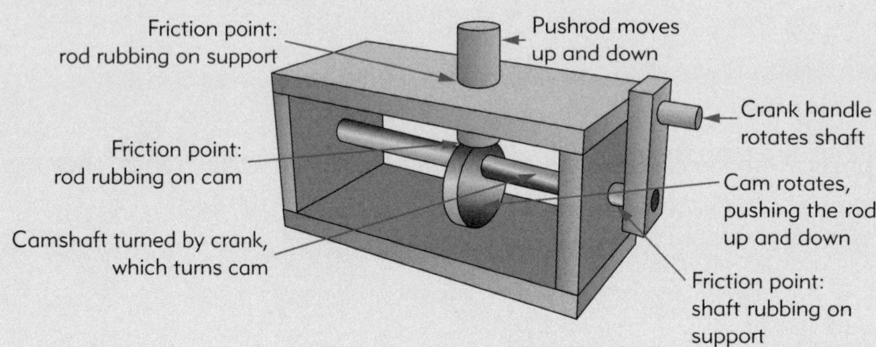

TASKS

To complete the Crank and Cam Automaton challenge, you need to carry out a range of design tasks. These can be done using Template B on page 137 in Part Three of this workbook, and by referring to pages 159–163 of the *Tech by Design Student Book*.

Your work should include (use this as a checklist – tick as you complete each task):

- ☐ A mind map exploring ideas and shapes for the moving part, materials to use, and who your automaton will be designed for.
- ☐ A design brief.
- ☐ Criteria for success – explaining what you expect in a good automaton.
  - Research into engineering basics – cams, cranks, rotary and reciprocal motion (pages 73–74).
  - Research into existing products and figurine ideas (page 74).
  - Research into pivots (page 75).
- ☐ Design sketches exploring shapes for all the parts and the entire automaton.
- ☐ A production plan to show the steps in constructing the product.
- ☐ A journal that records your production using photos and written reflections.
- ☐ An evaluation report using your criteria for success as a starting point.

RESEARCH – ENGINEERING BASICS

1 Complete Worksheet 4.3 in Part One of this workbook.

2 In small groups, discuss and define the following keywords. Write your definition and draw an illustration of each keyword in the space below.

KEYWORD	DEFINITION	DRAWING
Rotary motion		
Reciprocal motion		
Friction		
Cam		
Crank		

3 As a class, discuss the crank and cam image on page 71. What would be the effect of the following changes?

a Changing the length of the crank: ....

....

....

b Changing the cam from an eccentric cam to a snail cam: ....

....

....

RESEARCH – CHOOSING YOUR FIGURINE

1 Collect images and animations of hand-cranked wooden toys, and attach or draw them in the space below.

2 Refer to your collection and sketch parts that you could include in your automaton in the box below.

3 Consider the features of the products that you have sketched. How are they attached to the pushrod? Some will be complex. Draw further sketches to show how the parts could be attached simply for ease of construction.

 9780170400206

RESEARCH – PIVOTS

1 A moving part or figurine may be anchored to the top plate with one or more of its parts joined to the pushrod. Describe **three** different pivoting methods in the space below, and check with your teacher which of these pivot methods are possible in your school with the available tools and equipment.

- ....
- ....
- ....

2 Choose one of the pivoting methods from Question 1. Sketch and annotate to show how it could be used to pivot the moving parts on your automaton.

Use the Engineering template (B) starting on page 137 to complete your challenge.

CHALLENGE 6.2

PULL-ALONG AUTOMATON DESIGN CHALLENGE

DESIGN CHALLENGE 6.2: PULL-ALONG AUTOMATON

Children have enjoyed pushing and pulling toys since wheels were invented, and possibly even before that. Some of the best traditional toys contain parts that move with a turning axle. Each axle has a cam attached and pushes a pushrod. Design and create a moving toy that will bring joy to a child. Each axle of your toy will have a cam attached and will push a pushrod.

REQUIREMENTS (LIMITS OR CONSTRAINTS)

- The product size will be set by your teacher.
- Use the materials available in your school (or provide special materials from home).
- Your design must have a part or figurine moving back and forth or up and down as the toy is pulled along.
- The part or figurine must be moved by the cam on the axle as it turns.

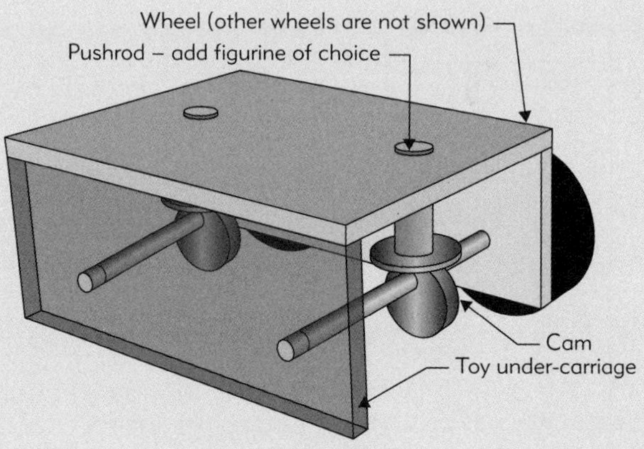

DESIGN CHOICES

You will need to make design decisions regarding:

- the shape and form of the under-carriage
- the design of the figurine that will be moving up and down on top of the toy
- further challenge: replace the cam with a crank.

TASKS

To complete the Pull-along Automaton challenge, you need to carry out a range of design tasks. These can be done using Template B on page 137 in Part Three of this workbook, and by referring to pages 159–163 of the *Tech by Design Student Book*.

Your work should include (use this as a checklist – tick as you complete each task):

- ☐ A mind map exploring aspects of the pull-along toy, the shape of the figurine and the cam.
- ☐ A design brief.
- ☐ Criteria for success – explaining what you expect your pull along toy to do, how it should look and the quality you would like to achieve.
  - Research into crankshafts and camshafts (page 77) and pushrods (page 78).
  - Research into existing products and toys.
- ☐ Design sketches exploring shapes, forms, colours, placement, proportions, etc.
- ☐ A production plan to show the steps in constructing the product.
- ☐ A journal that records your production using photos and written reflections.
- ☐ An evaluation report using your criteria for success as a starting point.

RESEARCH – CRANKSHAFT VS CAMSHAFT

1 Collect images and animations of crankshafts, and attach or draw them in the space below.

2 Describe the differences between crankshafts and camshafts.

3 Which drive shaft is best for your design? Crankshaft or camshaft?

RESEARCH – PUSHROD END

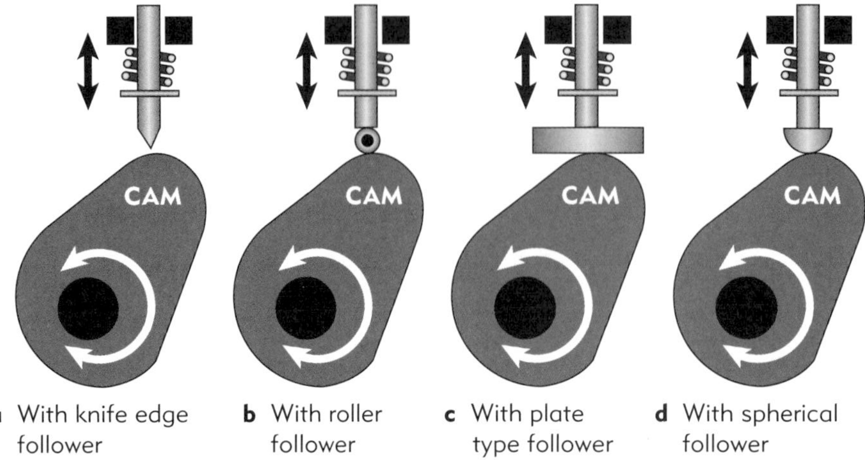

a With knife edge follower

b With roller follower

c With plate type follower

d With spherical follower

Varieties of pushrod ends available for your pull-along cam toy

Consider the ends of the four pushrods shown.

1 Which pushrod would be best for making good contact with the cam?

....

2 Which pushrod would have the lowest friction?

....

3 Which pushrod is most likely to jam?

....

4 What would happen if a plate-type pushrod was used and placed just off centre?

....

....

....

Use the Engineering template (B) starting on page 137 to complete your challenge.

CHALLENGE 6.3

FAIRGROUND MODEL DESIGN CHALLENGE

DESIGN CHALLENGE 6.3: FAIRGROUND MODEL

Theme parks and fairgrounds are full of amazing rides that children (and adults!) enjoy. Rides can vary in intensity, from gentle Ferris wheels to exciting roller-coasters. In this design challenge, you get to recreate the fun and drama of these rides. Design and create a working model of a fairground ride that allows the user to easily and comfortably control the speed.

REQUIREMENTS (LIMITS OR CONSTRAINTS)

- Your model must look great and feel smooth.
- The mechanism must move with low friction.
- The crank needs to move easily.
- Gears, a belt drive or a chain drive must be incorporated to change the speed.

DESIGN CHOICES

You will need to make design decisions regarding:

- type of ride to create and all its parts
- materials to use
- mechanisms to use (such as belt or chain drive).

TASKS

To complete the Fairground Model challenge, you need to carry out a range of design tasks. These can be done using Template B on page 137 in Part Three of this workbook, and by referring to pages 159–163 of the *Tech by Design Student Book*.

Your work should include (use this as a checklist – tick as you complete each task):

- [ ] A mind map exploring aspects of fairground rides, the number of people to seat, materials to use and other challenge requirements for your model.
- [ ] A design brief.
- [ ] Criteria for success for your model.
  - Research into chain and belt drives (page 80) and crank length (page 81).
  - Research into existing fairground rides.
  - Research into all the mechanisms that you will use.
- [ ] Design sketches exploring the structure of the ride, the seating, the mechanisms, their placement, etc.
- [ ] A production plan.
- [ ] A journal that records your production using photos and written reflections.
- [ ] An evaluation report using your criteria for success as a starting point.

RESEARCH – CHANGING DRIVE SPEED

Belt and chain drives are useful for a few reasons. Changing the length of the belt allows the drive to sit some distance away from the mechanism. Having the drive sitting away from the mechanism creates room to turn the crank without hitting your knuckles on the model. By changing the diameter of the pulleys or sprockets, you can make the ride rotate faster or slower than the turning of your crank. The drive is the origin of the movement that drives the ride – in this case a human hand or motor.

Investigate belt and pulley drives (page 124 of the *Tech by Design Student Book*) and then answer the questions below.

1 Complete the drawing of the belt and pulley system below by adding a pulley wheel that would make the ride go twice as slow as the driver pulley.

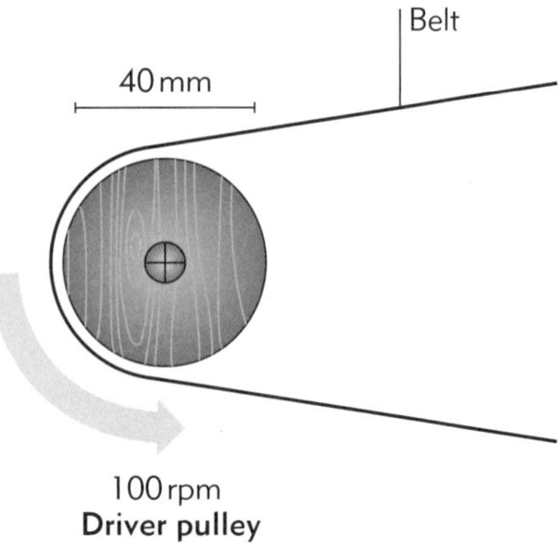

2 A chain and sprocket drive works in a very similar way to a belt drive. Give a reason why you might use a chain and sprocket instead of a pulley drive.

....

....

3 Give an example of a chain and sprocket used as a drive.

....

....

4 Give a reason why you might use a pulley drive instead of a chain and sprocket.

....

....

5 Give an example of a pulley system used as a drive.

....

....

RESEARCH – CHANGING CRANK LENGTH

Changing the length of a crank can make it easier to turn the pulley or sprocket system. Just as extending the length of a ratchet arm makes it easier to turn a bolt, the longer you make your crank handle, the easier it will be to turn.

1 Research wooden toys, fairground rides and the length of cranks used by other designers to find the optimal length. Use the space below for your research notes, and then record the length you have decided to use.

Chosen crank length: ....

2 What is the effect of doubling the length of a crank arm?

....

....

3 Use the space below to draw labelled diagrams to help you remember the names of all parts of pulley or sprocket systems and the effects of changing handle length.

Use the Engineering template (B) starting on page 137 to complete your challenge.

CHALLENGE 7.1

SWITCH-CONTROLLED ROBOT DESIGN CHALLENGE

DESIGN CHALLENGE 7.1: SWITCH-CONTROLLED ROBOT

Simple robots can be controlled to sense objects in the vicinity and move around them by moving backwards, forwards, turning, or spinning around. To do so, they need motors and wheels to drive them. All of the parts are securely housed on the chassis. Design and create a robot for a task (such as to play soccer), to move along a designated track, or another activity.

REQUIREMENTS (LIMITS OR CONSTRAINTS)

- The product should be no larger than the size set by your teacher.
- The motors and wheels must be well-aligned.
- The robot must move as the controls intend it to.
- Soldering must be checked before adding batteries (one bad connection can cause the batteries to overheat).

DESIGN CHOICES

You will need to make design decisions regarding:

- the shape and form of the robot, the chassis and hand controller
- shape, form, colour and position of the switches.

If your teacher advises that you have mastered the basics in this challenge, extend yourself with the harder DPDT-switched robot.

TASKS

To complete the Switch-controlled Robot challenge, you need to carry out a range of design tasks. These can be done using Template B on page 137 in Part Three of this workbook, and by referring to pages 173–176 of the *Tech by Design Student Book*.

Your work should include (use this as a checklist – tick as you complete each task):

- ☐ Activities that cover what you need to know about differential steering and switches (pages 83–85).
- ☐ A mind map or other graphic organiser to explore ways of constructing, moving and controlling the robot.
- ☐ A design brief.
- ☐ Criteria for success – explaining what you expect the robot to do and how it should look.
  - Research into switches, motors, batteries, gearboxes and wheels.
- ☐ Design sketches exploring ideas for your robot, chassis and hand controller, and the placement of parts.
- ☐ Working drawings of your chosen design.
- ☐ A list of all the mechanisms and electronic components required.
- ☐ A production plan to show the steps in constructing the product.
- ☐ A journal that records your production using photos and written reflections.
- ☐ An evaluation report using your criteria for success as a starting point.

INVESTIGATING SWITCHES

When constructing your switch-controlled robot, it is important to understand how a switch works (most commonly used are rocker or slide switches). Research SPST and DPDT switches and then answer the following questions to check your understanding.

SPST switches

1 What does SPST stand for?

....

2 Label all the parts of the SPST switch on the right to indicate the difference between the two positions.

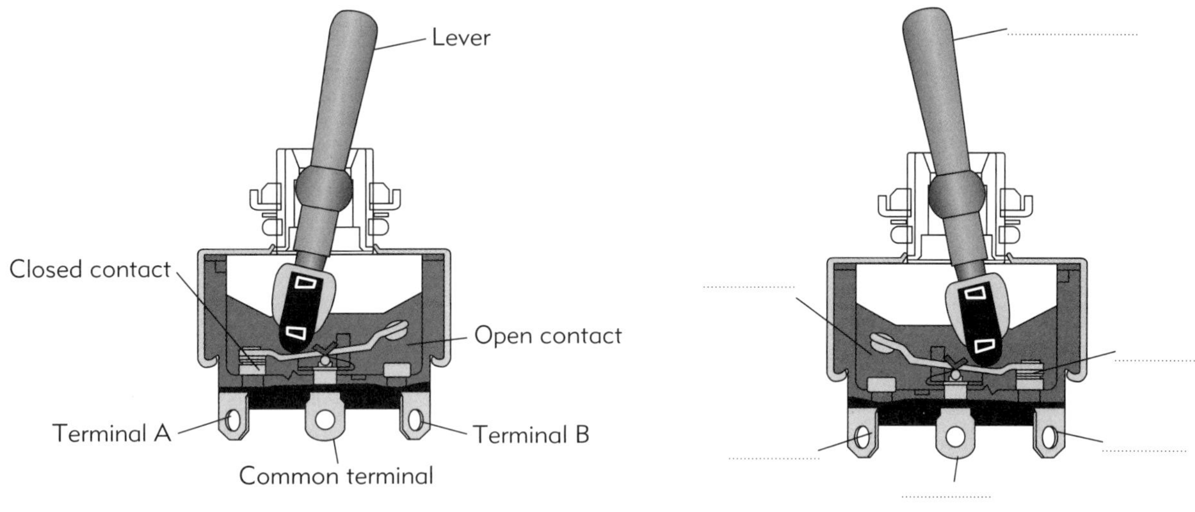

Common- and A-terminal connected | **Common- and B-terminal connected**

3 If you wish to use the switch above for the SPST challenge, only two terminals need to be used. Look at the labelled image to decide which terminal must be used. Hint: which terminal is used in both switching situations?

....

4 Look at the images above. Do terminals A and B ever connect?

....

5 a Collect an SPST switch and a multimeter. Set the multimeter to 'audible continuity'. Hold the probes on the A terminal and the common terminal. When the terminals are connected, the multimeter will make an audible beep.

b Complete the table below by writing 'beep' or 'no beep'. (A = terminal A, B = terminal B, C = common terminal).

LEVER TO THE LEFT	CONNECTED (BEEP?)	LEVER TO THE RIGHT	CONNECTED (BEEP?)
A – C		A – C	
A – B		B – C	

DPDT switches

For a DPDT (double-pole, double-throw) switch, two switches work in unison. In the images below, terminal C can only connect to either A or E, and terminal D can connect to B and F. Because there are two switches moving together, when terminal C connects to E, terminal D connects to F.

DPDT switch

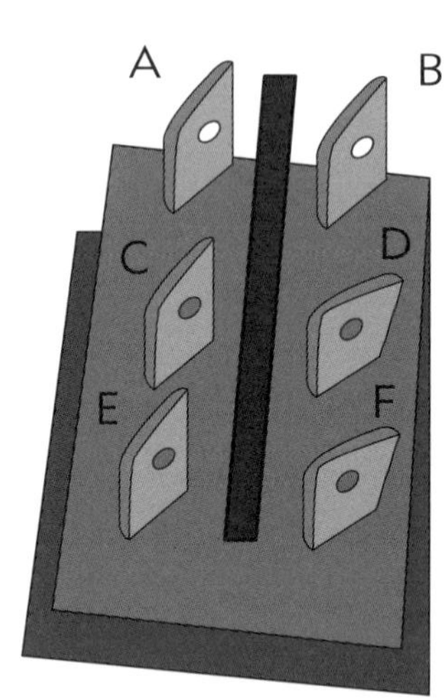

Underside of DPDT Switch

7 Set a multimeter to 'audible continuity' and complete the table to explain the connections of a DPDT switch. In each box write 'beep' or 'no beep'.

LEVER TO THE LEFT	CONNECTED (BEEP?)	LEVER TO THE RIGHT	CONNECTED (BEEP?)
A – C		A – C	
B – D		B – D	
C – E		C – E	
D – F		D – F	
A – E		A – E	
B – F		B – F	

DIFFERENTIAL STEERING ACTIVITY

The switch-controlled robot is powered and steered by only two motors using **differential** steering.

1 Research how differential steering works.

  9780170400206

2 Complete the table below by adding the words 'on' and 'off' to explain how differential steering works.

DIRECTION	LEFT MOTOR	RIGHT MOTOR
Forward		
Left		
Right	on	
Stop	off	

3 If you wanted a robot to follow the path shown from start to finish, list the order of steps (directions) and the switching you would need to do for each step in the table below. The first two steps have been completed for you.

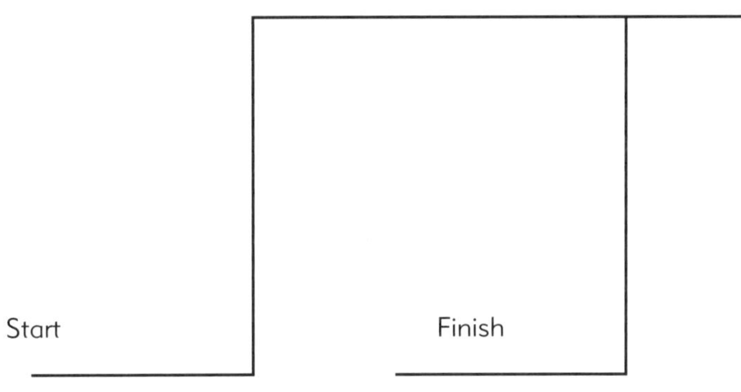

Forward ⟶

STEP DIRECTION	LEFT MOTOR	RIGHT MOTOR	DESCRIPTION
1.	on	on	forward
2.	off	on	turn left
3.			
4.			
5.			
6.			
7.			
8.			
9.			
10.			
11.			

Use the Engineering template (B) starting on page 137 to complete your challenge.

CHALLENGE
7.2

SENSOR-CONTROLLED ROBOT DESIGN CHALLENGE

DESIGN CHALLENGE 7.2: SENSOR-CONTROLLED ROBOT

Many robots have sensors that detect light from sources such as a torch or the sun. These sensors can initiate movement of the robot. Design and make a hands-free, light-sensoring wireless robot with a purpose such as getting you out of bed in the morning by noise or movement, or to entertain a child when he/she switches a torch off and on.

The robot you design will go on a chassis as described on pages 165–6 of the *Tech by Design* Student Book.

REQUIREMENTS (LIMITS OR CONSTRAINTS)

- Use the materials available in your school (or provide special materials from home).
- The robot must detect light.
- It must follow controls as intended.
- Soldering must be checked before adding batteries (batteries may overheat and be damaged if there is a mistake in wiring or soldering).

DESIGN CHOICES

You will need to make design decisions regarding:

- the shape and form of the robot, the chassis and hand controller
- how you will enhance the design of the chassis and hand controller.

TASKS

To complete the Sensor-controlled Robot challenge, you need to carry out a range of design tasks. These can be done using Template B on page 137 in Part Three of this workbook, and by referring to pages 173–176 of the *Tech by Design Student Book*.

Your work should include (use this as a checklist – tick as you complete each task):

- ☐ Activities that cover what you need to know about light-dependent resistors (LDRs) and trimpots (page 87).
- ☐ A mind map or other graphic organiser exploring aspects of the sensor-controlled robot challenge; e.g. movement, control, types of components.
- ☐ A design brief.
- ☐ Criteria for success – explaining what you expect your robot to do, with what precision and how it will look.
  - Research into resistors, light-dependent resistors (LDRs), transistors, diodes, motors, batteries and wheels.
- ☐ Design sketches.
- ☐ Working drawings of your chosen design.
- ☐ A list of all the mechanism parts and electronic components required.

- [ ] A production plan to show the steps in constructing the product.
- [ ] A journal that records your production using photos and written reflections.
- [ ] An evaluation report using your criteria for success as a starting point.

NOTE

Before starting the activities below, make sure you complete Worksheets 4.5–4.8 in Part One of this workbook.

INVESTIGATING LIGHT-DEPENDENT RESISTORS (LDRs)

An LDR changes its resistance depending on the intensity of the light it is exposed to.

1 Use a multimeter, set to 'resistance', to observe how the resistance changes in different light levels. Clip the probes to the legs of the LDR. Hold the LDR in different light conditions. Observe the multimeter readings, and record them in the following table.

LIGHT LEVEL	RESISTANCE SHOWN (Ω)
Quite dark	
Normal room light	
Torch light	
Full sunlight	
Other	

MULTIMETERS

Carefully look for Ω, kΩ and MΩ symbols when reading the meter. There is a BIG difference between 9 Ω and 9 MΩ!
If your multimeter auto-ranges, hold the probes steady on the component and give the multimeter time to finish automatically ranging before recording the answer.

If your multimeter does not auto-range, start with large resistance values and turn down the resistance settings until you find the smallest setting that displays a resistance value.

2 What did you notice about when and how the resistance readings changed?

....

....

INVESTIGATING THE TRIMPOT

Rotating the trimpot on your circuit board sets the light levels to which your robot will respond.

The trimpot is a small, variable resistor. The resistance from one leg to the middle leg varies as you turn the trimpot's dial. The value of the resistor can be measured across the two outside legs (shown in the image as A and B). This value can also be found by adding the resistance of the outside leg to the middle leg (A – C), and adding that value to the resistance from the middle leg to the other outside leg (C – B).

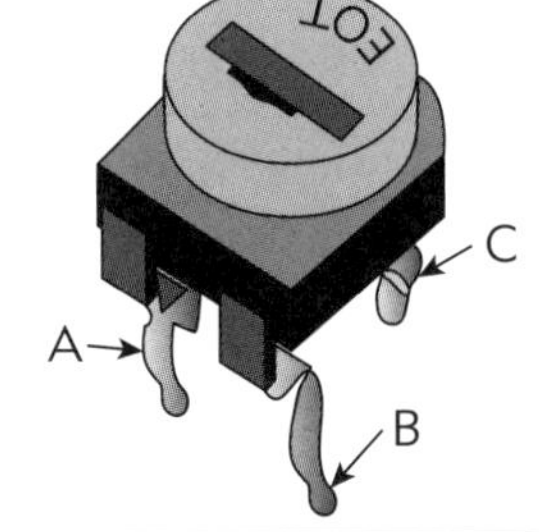

A trimpot

1 Use your multimeter to measure the resistance between the legs of the trimpot and complete the table.

TRIMPOT POSITION	A-C RESISTANCE IN Ω	B-C RESISTANCE IN Ω	ADD THE LAST TWO VALUES
Midpoint			
Turned right			
Turned left			

Use the Engineering template (B) starting on page 137 to complete your challenge.

CHALLENGE 7.3

ARDUINO-CONTROLLED ROBOT DESIGN CHALLENGE (EXTENSION)

DESIGN CHALLENGE 7.3: ARDUINO-CONTROLLED ROBOT

Advanced robots have their own onboard computers called microcontrollers. The robot you create in this challenge will go on a chassis as described on pages 165–6 in the *Tech by Design* Student Book.

You will need an Arduino Uno microcontroller, a motor-controller module, Arduino software installed on your computer and a download cable.

REQUIREMENTS (LIMITS OR CONSTRAINTS)

- The robot must respond as expected.

DESIGN CHOICES

You will need to make design and technical decisions regarding:

- the purpose of your robot
- the chassis shape and form, and materials used
- the power of your robot (battery packs can vary from 5 to 12 volt).

TASKS

To complete the Arduino-controlled Robot challenge, you need to carry out a range of design tasks. These can be done using Template B on page 137 in Part Three of this workbook, and by referring to pages 173–176 of the *Tech by Design Student Book*.

Your work should include (use this as a checklist – tick as you complete each task):

- ☐ Arduino Uno activities (page 89) and understanding code (pages 89–90).
- ☐ A mind map or other graphic organiser exploring aspects of the challenge; e.g. the mechanisms that could be used, what the robot could be used for.
- ☐ A design brief explaining the purpose and function of the robot.
- ☐ Criteria for success – explaining what you expect the robot to do, how it should look and its quality.
  - Research into an Arduino Uno, L298 motor modules, motors, batteries gearboxes and wheels.
- ☐ Design sketches of ideas for how the robot will look, and a construction or working drawing.
- ☐ A list of all the mechanism parts and electronic components required.
- ☐ A production plan to show the steps in constructing the product.
- ☐ A journal that records your production using photos and written reflections.
- ☐ An evaluation report discussing how well your robot works, whether it looks good and is fun to use.

USING ARDUINO UNO

You can find instructions to construct your robot on pages 171–3 of the *Tech by Design Student Book*.

However, before you construct your robot, it is important to familiarise yourself with the Arduino Uno micro-processor by following the instructions below.

An Arduino Uno micro-processor

On the image above:

1 Find pins 2–12 and label them digital input and output. You will use these pins to run your motors.

2 Find pins 10 and 11. Note the ~ symbol. These are two pins that can be used to change the speed of the motor. Label the PWM. (PWM stands for pulse width modulate.)

3 Label the external power supply on the bottom left of the Arduino 12V. This is where the batteries are connected.

4 Label the silver rectangle on the top left USB. The input program for the robot goes through this point.

UNDERSTANDING THE CODE

The following lines of code are explained in the table on the next page. Check your understanding by answering the questions after the table.

```
void setup() {
  // initialise digital pin 10 as an output
  pinMode (10, OUTPUT);
}

  // the loop function runs over and over again forever
void loop() {
  digitalWrite (10, HIGH);     // turn the LED on (HIGH is the voltage level)
  delay (2000);                // wait for 2 seconds
  digitalWrite (10, LOW);      // turn the LED off by making the voltage LOW
  delay (500);                 // wait for half a second
}
```

Note: Curly brackets start and finish both the void setup and void loop.

Line 1	: void setup() void setup() code only runs once and is used to tell the Arduino which pins will be outputs and to initialise those pins.
Line 2	: // Two forward slashes indicates a comment. The comments are not sent to the Arduino, they are just there to explain our code to other users.
Line 3	pinMode (10, OUTPUT); We initialise pin 10 as an output.
Line 5	A blank line is common between the void setup and void loop.
Line 7	void loop() Everything in the void loop repeats continuously and forever unless you turn off the Arduino.
Line 8	digitalWrite (10, HIGH); digitalWrite is used to turn the LED on. digitalWrite makes the Arduino supply 5 volts to pin 10 to turn the LED on.
Line 9	delay(2000); We keep the LED on for two seconds with this line:
Line 10	digitalWrite (10, LOW); digitalWrite is used to turn the LED off. digitalWrite makes the Arduino supply 0 volts to pin 10 and turns the LED off.
Line 11	delay(500); We keep the LED off for half a second with this line:
Line 12	} Has the curly bracket that indicates that void loop is over, and sends the program back to the top of void loop to repeat again.

1 What does the code 'void setup' do?

....

2 What does // do?

....

3 What does the code 'void loop' do?

....

4 Which line of code turns on the LED? ....

5 How do you write 'a delay of 2 seconds'? ....

NOTE

The Arduino online tutorials at Arduino.cc will help you learn more about Arduino before you tackle this challenge.

Use the Engineering template (B) starting on page 137 to complete your challenge.

9780170400206

CHALLENGE
8.1

HOUSE-IT DESIGN CHALLENGE

DESIGN CHALLENGE 8.1: HOUSE-IT

Design and make a shelter to house an animal.

REQUIREMENTS (LIMITS OR CONSTRAINTS)

- You need to make a feature of (showcase) your accuracy in one joining method or process (discuss this with your teacher).
- You must include other joining methods specified by your teacher.
- Joins must be accurate to 2 mm or less.
- Use the materials specified by your teacher (or provide special materials from home).
- You must include a roof, flap, or closable lid or door (discuss this with your teacher).
- The shelter needs to be aesthetically pleasing and professional-looking.

DESIGN CHOICES

You will need to make design decisions regarding:

- what animal your shelter is for (pet or wildlife)
- the form, shape and colour of your shelter
- how it will work
- the materials to use
- the joining method or process you will showcase.

TASKS

To complete the House-it challenge, you need to carry out a range of design tasks. These can be done using Template A on page 129 in Part Three of this workbook, and by referring to Chapter 8 of the *Tech by Design Student Book*.

Ask your teacher what tasks should be included from the list below (use this as a checklist – tick as you complete each task):

- ☐ Activity to brainstorm and select the animal (page 92).
- ☐ A graphic organiser to define the challenge in more detail (page 93).
- ☐ A design brief with four criteria for success.
- ☐ Research (insert into template and annotate):
  - the habits and needs of the animal
  - images of existing shelters; roofs, flaps, doors from any object
  - suitable materials and their availability, size, etc.
  - methods to attach the lid, flap or door
  - techniques for accuracy in your featured join (the one you are showcasing).
- ☐ Idea sketches and notes (in template) for:
  - different shapes, lids, flaps, doors, handles, windows, etc. for your shelter design
  - where the featured join will go.

- [ ] Refining and deciding on details (in template): combine your best ideas into one or two final designs, justify your final design, and create a 2D working drawing.
- [ ] Trial two joins and take photos to show how the quality of your work improved (attach to the template).
- [ ] Create a work plan (insert or attach into the template) that:
  - covers the main processes involved, including how the flap, lid or door will be attached
  - gives a timeline for each process to be completed
  - lists the materials
  - includes risk management.
- [ ] Make your shelter, following all safety precautions, and record your production work in the journal page (of the template); insert photos if you have them.
- [ ] Evaluate by presenting your finished product to the class, explaining how it met the criteria for success (write this out in the template first).
- [ ] On a separate blank page, draw a diagram of your featured process, or insert a close-up photo; annotate to suggest how you could improve the quality of your work next time.

INVESTIGATING – BRAINSTORMING DIFFERENT ANIMALS AND THEIR SHELTERS

1 In pairs or in a group, discuss the different animals that you know require shelter.

2 In the chart below, list **four** animals from your discussion that you could realistically design and make shelter for. In the surrounding boxes, add any shelter that you know exists for each animal and list some exciting features you could include.

Animal 1

Animal 2

Animal 3

Animal 4

INVESTIGATING – DEFINE THE CHALLENGE AND GATHERING IDEAS

1 From your list of animals, choose the animal you are most likely to design and create shelter for. Create a mind map on a separate page showing how you could protect the animal, the ideas that you could take from existing shelters, and what interesting features you could add to improve them.

2 In the table below, draw and explain two ideas for a shelter with a roof, flap, lid or door that you like and could use from existing shelters for your chosen animal.

SHELTER 1	SHELTER 2
It protects	It protects
The ideas about this shelter that I like are:	The ideas about this shelter that I like are:

Draw **two** or **three** diagrams/sketches of how the flap, lid, roof or door is attached to the shelter. Annotate to explain how it moves and its purpose (i.e. to keep rain the off, to allow the animal in and out).

Use the General template (A) starting on page 129 to complete your challenge.

CHALLENGE
8.2

CLOTHE-IT DESIGN CHALLENGE

DESIGN CHALLENGE 8.2: CLOTHE-IT

Design and make an item of clothing for yourself or a pet to protect from the elements or a dangerous situation.

REQUIREMENTS (LIMITS OR CONSTRAINTS)

- The clothing item must be comfortable.
- Your design must include a fastener of some sort.
- There must be two different types of seams.
- All seams (or joins) must be straight and accurate.
- The clothing needs to be aesthetically pleasing and professional-looking.

DESIGN CHOICES

You will need to make design decisions regarding:

- what the clothing will protect you or your pet from (weather or a hazard)
- how it will fasten (ties, press studs, buttons, zipper, hook and eye, etc.)
- The material to use (cotton, leather, wool, PVC, etc.)
- The colours, shapes, textures and form of the clothing.

TASKS

To complete the Clothe-it challenge, you need to carry out a range of design tasks. These can be done using Template A on page 129 in Part Three of this workbook, and by referring to Chapter 8 of the *Tech by Design Student Book*.

Ask your teacher what tasks should be included from the list below (use this as a checklist – tick as you complete each task):

- [ ] Activity to brainstorm protective clothing to design and make for yourself or an animal (pages 95–96).
- [ ] A graphic organiser to define the challenge (any from this book can be drawn, or use the first space in the template): who are you designing for and what will it protect them from?
- [ ] A design brief with four criteria for success.
- [ ] Research (insert into template and annotate):
  - relevant sizes and facts (of the animal, the user or yourself) and some requirements of the clothing to be protective; images of similar clothing; suitable materials: availability, colours, cost, etc.; different fasteners; two seams (or knitting stitches) that your teacher has specified; and techniques for quality.
- [ ] Idea sketches and notes (in template) for:
  - suitable clothing designs; different fasteners and where they will be positioned on the clothing; ideas on colour, shape and texture combinations.
- [ ] Refining and deciding on details (in template): create two design options, justify your final design, and create a 2D 'flat' drawing with measurements, or a grid if using a knitting pattern.

- [ ] Practise two seams, methods of attaching fasteners, or knitting stitches until they are straight, with no mistakes or missed bits, no bunching of sewing thread, and with a suitable allowance for any seams; take photos to show how the quality of your work improved in each trial; write out step-by-step instructions for achieving quality in these methods (attach to the template).
- [ ] Create a scheduled plan (insert or attach into the template) that:
  - covers the main processes involved, provides extra details on how the fastener and any embellishment will be attached, details how to tidy up the work as a finished piece (sew in and cut loose threads, iron, etc.), gives a timeline for each process to be completed, lists the materials and includes risk management.
- [ ] Make your clothing pieces, following all safety precautions, and record your production work in the journal page (of the template); insert photos if you have them; if possible, include a photo of the clothing being worn by the user in your last journal entry.
- [ ] Evaluate by presenting your finished product to the class, explaining how it met the criteria for success (write this out in the template first); show the photo of the user and explain how your clothing fits them and is protective.
- [ ] On a separate blank page, draw a diagram or insert a close-up photo of the fastener you used and show how you attached it; annotate to suggest how you could improve the quality of your work next time.

INVESTIGATING IDEAS – DESIGN FOR A HUMAN OR ANIMAL

1 In pairs, discuss and compare:

- your favourite protective clothing/equipment – what did it protect you from? (e.g. weather or injury)
- protective clothing for animals and possible protective clothing you could design and make for yourself or an animal with the materials available to you.

2 Draw one of the clothing items you discussed that interests you (in the box on the left), and where it is worn for protection (in the box on the right). Annotate and use arrows to explain to your partner how it 'works' to protect, what you like about its design (the way it looks), the material it is made of, and when it is worn.

3 In the space below, make a sketch/diagram of the fasteners you discussed and could include in your design. Annotate how the fastener/s work.

4 Circle any of the animals (including the human, or add another animal) you might want to design for. In the circles below, brainstorm ideas for clothing you could design and what it could protect the wearer from. Draw a line to join the animal to the corresponding circles.

5 Select the animal or person that you will design and make protective clothing for. Create your own graphic organiser to define the who, what, what for, where and why questions for your design brief.

Use the General template starting on page 129 to complete your challenge.

Challenges 9.1–9.3 are focused on the needs of the Codo village in Timor Leste. It is important to investigate the context of these design challenges to create appropriate solutions. Read the information on pages 190–195 of the *Tech by Design* Student Book, or look for detailed information about other communities with similar needs. These challenges can be completed by **small groups** of students.

CLEAN WATER DESIGN CHALLENGE

DESIGN CHALLENGE 9.1: CLEAN WATER

Develop a method to purify water that comes from typical village drinking taps.

REQUIREMENTS

Although there are a range of things that could be done to improve the entire process of getting drinkable water to people in their homes, your team is being asked to concentrate on making the water drinkable once it gets there.

- Your team needs to develop a solution that will purify the water effectively.
- You will need to test your ideas, and assess whether a difference has been made.
- Your solution needs to be easy to use and durable.

DESIGN CHOICES

You need to decide on:

- suitable materials from those that are readily available
- the most suitable form of manufacturing and construction that is available
- the shape, form and functional aspects of the water purifier
- construction methods that allow the filter to be cleaned.

Your team can make a model or prototype from alternative materials if you do not have access to the materials suitable for your design.

TASKS

You will be completing the Clean Water challenge in a group. To do this, you will need to carry out a range of design tasks using Template C on page 143 in Part Three of this workbook. Your work should include (use this as a checklist – tick as you complete each task):

- ☐ A discovery task that considers the specific water needs of people in the Codo village (page 98).
- ☐ A design brief explaining why the Codo people need a new water system and water purification, and the limitations of the setting.
- ☐ Criteria for success – explaining what you expect in a good clean water solution.
- ☐ Research into existing solutions (page 98), Purifying Water trials (page 99), and materials research.
- ☐ Design sketches and design options describing your ideas and possible solutions.
- ☐ A model or mock-up of your most suitable design.
- ☐ An evaluation report that assess how well your final solution suits the needs of the community.

DISCOVERY TASK

Read pages 190–195 of the *Tech by Design* Student Book explaining the water situation in Codo, Timor-Leste. Alternatively, conduct an internet search on 'clean water issues' to find out about other communities also suffering because they don't have access to clean water.

As a group, research, discuss and answer the following questions:

1 Explain the difference between the way water is delivered to homes in Codo (or another community you researched) and the way it is delivered to your home.

....

....

2 Explain the difference between the quality of water from Codo and your home.

....

....

3 What are the consequences of drinking poor quality water?

....

....

4 List **two** ways a water system delivering poor quality water could be improved.

....

....

5 What are some issues that arise from the situation in Timor-Leste (or your researched community) that might make a new water delivery system or the changes in behaviour required to use a water purifier difficult?

....

....

WHAT SOLUTIONS ARE ALREADY OUT THERE?

Find a solution for a water delivery system or a water purifier that has already been developed to provide clean water to disadvantaged communities. Research and develop a brief class presentation that explains this solution. Cover the following points:

- What does it look like and what are its features?
- Who is it mainly designed for?
- How does it work?
- Advantages/disadvantages of the system?
- Who developed it?

NOTE

Some existing solutions include:

- the life straw
- the life sack
- play pumps (pumping water)
- the Q drum (moving water)
- the tippy tap (hygiene).

  9780170400206

PURIFYING WATER

There are five stages of water purification – aeration, flocculation, sedimentation and filtration and disinfection. In this activity, you will investigate the first four methods. Using dirty water, different groups can experiment with the order of the filtration materials. Because you are not disinfecting the water (the final stage of the water purification process), remember that your water **isn't safe to drink** after your experiment.

TIP

Search the internet for the video 'Water Filtration Experiment'. This explains how to filter water in more detail.

1 Find or create 2 litres of 'dirty' water (e.g. mix tap water with dirt or mud)

2 Aerate the water by shaking in a bottle and pouring from container to container many times.

3 Mix a teaspoon of alum into the water. Stir for 5 minutes. (Flocculation)

4 Allow to stand for 20 minutes. (Sedimentation)

5 Use the materials listed to create a water filter. Pour the water through your filter.

- 2 litres of dirty water
- empty soft drink bottles
- large beaker or jar
- pebbles
- course sand
- fine sand
- activated carbon (from pet stores)

Your research should guide you in deciding which order to place your materials in your final solution. Record your observations by completing the following.

a Describe what your water was like when you started.

....

b In the following table, describe how you carried out each of the four stages of purification, explain the purpose of each stage and note your observations.

STAGE	DESCRIPTION	PURPOSE	OBSERVATION
Aeration			
Flocculation			
Sedimentation			
Filtration			

c Describe what your water looked like at the end of each of the four stages.

d How could carbon or ceramic help you to purify water?

e Research and briefly describe two ways you can use the sun and ultraviolet rays (UV) to purify water.

f What chemicals are used to disinfect water?

g How could you use this information to develop a clean water solution?

Use the Group work template (C) starting on page 143 to complete your challenge.

 9780170400206

APPROPRIATE HOUSING DESIGN CHALLENGE

DESIGN CHALLENGE 9.2: APPROPRIATE HOUSING

As a team, you are challenged to design and create a model house for a family in Codo village.

REQUIREMENTS

Your team needs to consider the following:

- Local materials are preferred as imported materials are very expensive.
- The house needs to withstand extreme weather and possible earthquakes.
- The house needs to be protected from heat, wind and rain.
- The house needs to be simple to build.

DESIGN CHOICES

Your team needs to explore and make decisions about:

- materials that are the most cost-effective (work well for the least amount of money)
- materials that give the best results in terms of protection and strength
- house shapes and structures that best suit the conditions
- types of construction techniques that are simple and do not require electrical tools.

TASKS

You will be completing this design challenge in a group. To do this, you will need to carry out a range of design tasks using Template C on page 143 in Part Three of this workbook.

Your work should include (use this as a checklist – tick as you complete each task):

- ☐ A discovery task that considers the building needs of people in the Lautém region (pages 101–102).
- ☐ A design brief explaining the need for better housing, and the limitations of the setting.
- ☐ Criteria for success – explaining what you expect in a good housing solution.
- ☐ Building material trial (pages 103–105).
- ☐ Research into materials or joins, existing products (houses) and suitable roof shapes.
- ☐ Design sketches of your ideas and design options describing more complete solutions.
- ☐ A model of your best solution.
- ☐ An evaluation report that assess how well your solution meets the needs of the situation.

DISCOVERY TASK

Read the information about the housing issues of the people in the Lautém region (pages 193–195) of the *Tech by Design Student Book*. Alternatively, read about some other housing projects and programs. Internet searches for 'Engineers Without Borders', 'Habitat for Humanity' and 'Community Housing Ltd' are good places to start.

APPROPRIATE HOUSING DESIGN CHALLENGE

Discuss either the section in the *Tech by Design* Student Book or online information to answer the following questions.

1 How is your house different from the houses in Lautém (or another disadvantaged area)?

2 What is the climate like there?

3 Describe one of the traditional houses you've seen – discuss the materials used, the shape, the size, how it is positioned on the land, its roof, windows and doors, etc. Draw the house in the space below and write descriptive comments.

4 Why do you think this traditional house is built the way it is?

5 Where do you think the materials come from to build these houses?

6 What are some of the problems and issues you would face if you tried to build a new house in this area?

9780170400206

TESTING DIFFERENT BUILDING MATERIALS – GROUP ACTIVITY

1 A house provides protection. In a small group, discuss what natural things a house protects you from and list these below.

2 List the main materials that could be used to build house walls and roofing in the Lautém region (consider what they use now, and what other materials could be used). Using the discussions you've had in your group and your experience, complete the following table about the advantages and disadvantages of each material (remember that access to the Lautém area is difficult).

MATERIAL	ADVANTAGE	DISADVANTAGE

3 Simulate (copy as closely as possible) and test two wall materials and two roofing materials to find out which materials give the best protection from heat.

You will need:

- wall suggestions: clay/mud (can have some grass added for strength) and timber (straight sticks stuck together); you can use different materials if you can find better alternatives
- roofing suggestions: long thick grass (bound together in small clumps) and metal (thin aluminium such as a disposable baking tray); you can use different materials if you can find better alternatives
- heat – you will need something that produces heat (a hairdryer or heater), or place the models outside on a hot day
- digital thermometer

SAFETY NOTE

Safety will be an issue, so conduct your testing under supervision from your teacher. Make sure you don't heat the materials up too much in case they catch fire.

4 Make your model houses – you will need to make four of the same size and shape (the size of a shoebox would be a good template to use). Construct the roof structure so that it is freestanding and can be swapped from one wall structure to another.

Draw pictures or attach photos of your 'houses'.

HOUSE A	
Wall 1	Roof 1

HOUSE B	
Wall 2	Roof 2

HOUSE C	
Wall 1	Roof 2

HOUSE D	
Wall 2	Roof 1

5 Place houses A and B in a hot area. Record the temperature within the houses every 5 minutes over a period of 20 minutes.

6 Allow your houses to cool, and then swap the roofing material. Repeat step 5 for houses C and D.

Record all your results in the following table.

HOUSE	MATERIALS		TEMPERATURE			
	WALL	ROOF	5 MINS	10 MINS	15 MINS	20 MINS
A						
B						
C						
D						

What did you notice about the temperatures you recorded?

....

....

7 Which materials do your results suggest might be better for housing construction? Explain why.

- Walls ....

....

- Roof ....

....

8 This test will only give you an indication of the best materials. Why might your test be inaccurate or invalid? How does it differ from a real-life situation?

....

....

....

....

....

9 How could you improve your test?

....

....

....

....

....

....

Use the Group work template (C) starting on page 143 to complete your challenge.

CHALLENGE 9.3

CHILD-FRIENDLY PLAY AREA DESIGN CHALLENGE

DESIGN CHALLENGE 9.3: CHILD-FRIENDLY PLAY AREA

REQUIREMENTS

Design a play area for the Lautém Child-Friendly Space (near Codo) that is safe, fun and educational for children aged 2–5 years old. Consider the following limitations and requirements of the situation when designing your play area.

- There is little or no money available for building the play area.
- The equipment must be safe for young children.
- Volunteers will build the play area (both local volunteers and partner organisations overseas).
- There is limited access to electricity for construction.

DESIGN CHOICES

Your team needs to consider:

- the types of activities/equipment that can be fun and educational
- the materials that are locally available
- how to make it simple to construct with hand tools.

TASKS

You will be completing the Child-friendly Play Area challenge in a group. To do this, you will need to carry out a range of design tasks using Template C on page 143 in Part Three of this workbook.

Your work should include (use this as a checklist – tick as you complete each task):

- ☐ A discovery task that considers the playground needs of children in Lautém (read the background on page 197 of the *Tech by Design* Student Book).
- ☐ A design brief explaining the need for a safe space for children to play in, and the limitations of the setting.
- ☐ Criteria for success – explaining what you expect in a good playground solution.
- ☐ Playground research (pages 107–108).
- ☐ Research into joins Activity 3.9 or materials, including recycled materials (Activities 2.1, 2.3 or 2.4).
- ☐ Design sketches of your initial ideas and design options showing more complete solutions.
- ☐ A model of your most suitable design option.
- ☐ An evaluation report that assesses how well your solution solves the 'problem'.

WHAT MAKES A GOOD PLAYGROUND?

1 Look at the two photos below and comment on their good and 'not-so-good' features.

PLAYGROUND 1	PLAYGROUND 2
Shutterstock.com/Nikolai Lan	Shutterstock.com/francesco de marco
Good	Good
Not-so-good	Not-so-good

2 Talk to a number of small children about the things they like, and don't like, about the playgrounds they use. Ask about particular equipment, and the level of challenge (how hard it is to do things). You could arrange to visit your local primary school to do this. Record their comments here.

EQUIPMENT THEY LIKE:	LEVEL OF CHALLENGE OR DIFFICULTY:	FEATURES THEY DISLIKE:

3 What are the best things you remember about the playgrounds you used as a little child?

4 How do you make a playground safe? What features did you see in the playgrounds you investigated that made them safe for children to play in?

Use the Group work template (C) starting on page 143 to complete your challenge.

RECYCLE A PALLET DESIGN CHALLENGE

DESIGN CHALLENGE 10.1: RECYCLE A PALLET

Use an existing pallet to design and make a new, useful product.

REQUIREMENTS (LIMITS OR CONSTRAINTS)

- Your product needs to be made from a certain percentage of pallet pieces, as specified by your teacher.
- You can combine your product with other materials, as specified by your teacher (or provide materials and components from home).
- You must include wood joints other than butt joints, as specified by your teacher.

DESIGN CHOICES

You will need to make decisions regarding:

- the product to make, its purpose and the user
- how to improve the aesthetics of the used pallet pieces (either by decoration, fine sanding, or emphasis on faults)
- any decorative element (such as holes, carving, plywood shapes, or acrylic additions)
- other components you might add.

TASKS

To complete the Recycle a Pallet challenge, you need to carry out a range of design tasks. These can be done using Template A on page 129 in Part Three of this workbook, and by referring to Chapter 10 of the *Tech by Design Student Book*.

Ask your teacher what tasks should be included from the list below (use this as a checklist – tick as you complete each task):

- ☐ An annotated image of the pallet you will be re-using (pages 110–111) to explain parts, the material it is made from and how the parts are joined.
- ☐ A list of the processes you will be able to complete with the equipment available to you.
- ☐ Disassemble the pallet, clean up the pieces, and create a visual list (page 111) of the dimensions of all the pallet pieces you can use (include length, width and thickness).
- ☐ Brainstorm (in your template) the product type and aesthetic decisions you could make.
- ☐ A design brief (in template) that starts with: '*The pallet I am re-using is made of … I am going to use the material to design and make a … for …*'
- ☐ Create four criteria for success related to aesthetics, suitability or usefulness to the user, the quality of the product and its safety.
- ☐ Research (insert in your template):
  - images of existing similar products or the use of recycled pallets, with annotations to explain how you could use these ideas.

- [ ] Idea sketches and notes (in your template) for the product design, decorative shapes to add and what joins to use, taking into account your pallet pieces and their sizes; create one final design drawing (in your template), annotate, and create a 2D working drawing with dimensions.
- [ ] Trial two processes on scrap pallet pieces, and take photos to show how the quality of your work improved (attach to the template).
- [ ] Create a work plan that:
  - covers the main processes involved, including how any decoration will be attached,
  - gives a timeline to complete each process and includes risk management.

  (Insert or attach all your plans into the template.)
- [ ] Make your product, following all safety precautions, and record your production work in the journal page (of your template); insert photos.
- [ ] Evaluate by writing your criteria for success (in your template), checking the product and giving your opinion, particularly on its safety. Comment on the processes involved, any trials that helped, what you enjoyed, and what was difficult about working with and planning around pre-used material in limited sizes. Make suggestions for others attempting this task.

ANNOTATING THE EXISTING PALLET

1 Insert an image or diagram of your pallet in the centre frame below.

2 Annotate the parts (the stringers and the deck boards), the name of the material (pine, hardwood, etc.), and how the parts are joined (stapled, nailed, etc.). The annotations are partially completed for you. You need to extend the lines to indicate where they are on your image.

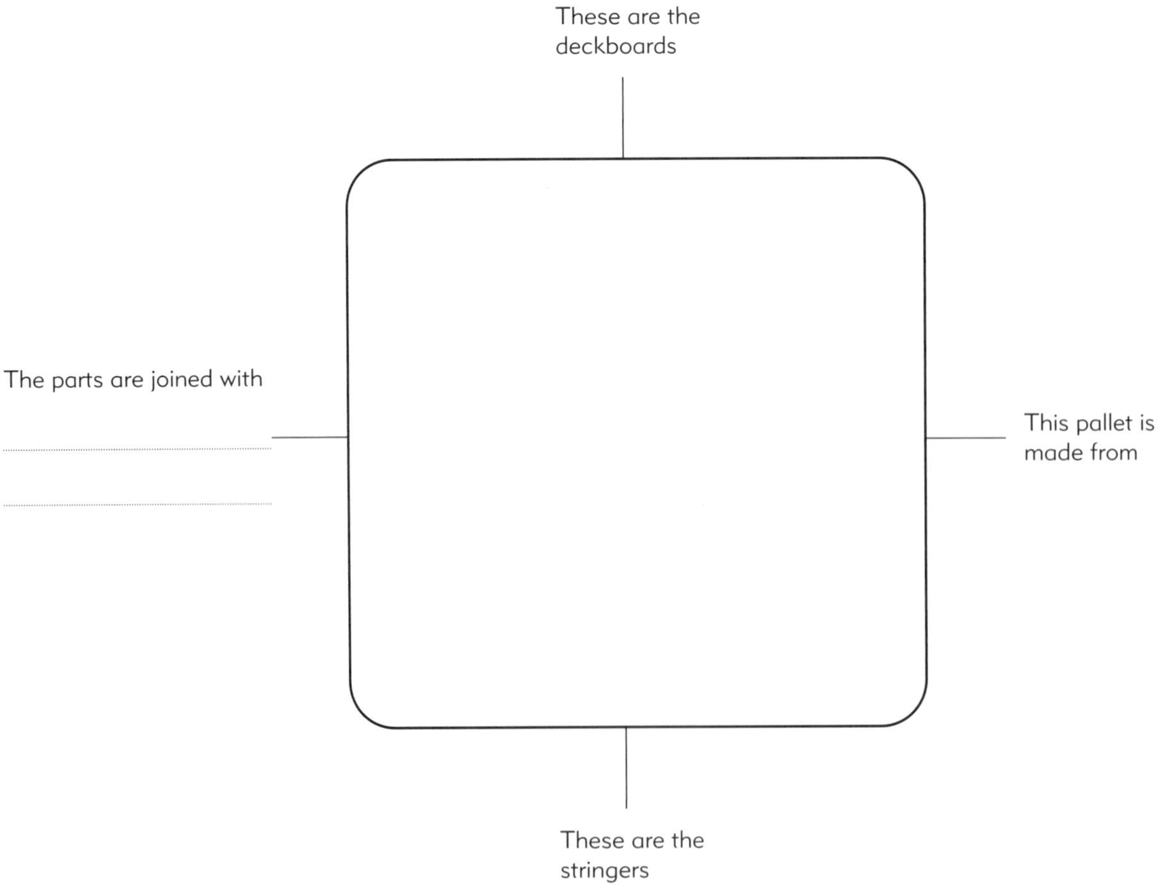

PREPARING THE PALLET

1 In the following table, write a list of the processes needed to 'clean up' your pallet pieces, and the equipment you need to do so.

PROCESSES (MEASURING, MARKING, CUTTING, DRILLING, JOINING, ATTACHING, GLUING, RASPING, FILING, SANDING, ETC.)	EQUIPMENT I CAN USE

2 Once the pallet is disassembled and pieces are cleaned up, use the table below (which has been scaled from 0–1200 mm) to create a visual list of the dimensions of all the pallet pieces you can use. Include the length, width and thickness. Draw the longest pieces at the top of the table.

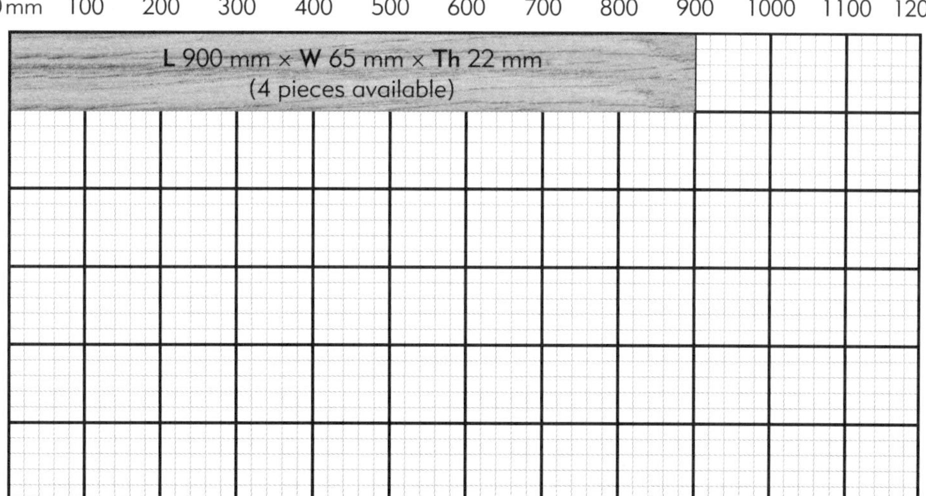

Add more rows to the table if needed.

Continue with the tasks (outlined at the start of the challenge) using Template A.

Use the General template (A) starting on page 129 to complete your challenge.

CHALLENGE 10.2

RE-USE A PAIR OF JEANS DESIGN CHALLENGE

DESIGN CHALLENGE 10.2: RE-USE A PAIR OF JEANS

Use an existing pair of jeans and turn them into a new, useful product.

REQUIREMENTS (LIMITS OR CONSTRAINTS)

- Your product needs to be made from a pair of jeans.
- You can combine it with other materials, as specified by your teacher (or provide materials and components from home).
- You must include a fastener and other **embellishment** processes, as specified by your teacher.

DESIGN CHOICES

You will need to make decisions regarding:

- the product to make, its purpose and the user
- the type of fastener and whether embellishments will be functional or decorative
- the types of seams
- other fabric or components you might add (such as buckles, buttons, press studs, etc.).

TASKS

To complete the Re-use a Pair of Jeans challenge, you need to carry out a range of design tasks. These can be done using Template A on page 129 in Part Three of this workbook, and by referring to Chapter 10 of the *Tech by Design Student Book*.

Ask your teacher what tasks should be included from the list below (use this as a checklist – tick as you complete each task):

- ☐ Learn about denim (pages 113–114).
- ☐ A graph to show a small survey on jeans ownership; and an annotated analysis of the jeans you are re-using (page 114).
- ☐ A mind map of possible products to make and processes to include.
- ☐ A design brief (in the template) with four 'criteria for success'.
- ☐ Research (insert into template and annotate):
  - images of inspiring products and uses for recycled denim
  - different processes to include (specified by your teacher) and techniques for quality.
- ☐ Idea sketches and notes (in your template):
  - different processes, fasteners, embroidery or applique, and where they will be positioned
  - ideas on shape, texture and combinations with other materials, or any different colours.
- ☐ Refining and deciding on details (in template): create two design options, justify your final design, and create a 2D 'flat' drawing with measurements.

9780170400206

☐ Practise two processes on scrap, such as methods of attaching fasteners, embroidery or applique, until they are accurate or straight, with no mistakes or missed bits, no bunching of sewing thread, and using a suitable thread colour; take photos to show how the quality of your work improved in each trial; write out step-by-step instructions for achieving quality in these methods (attach to the template).

☐ Create a scheduled plan (insert or attach into the template) that:

- covers the main processes involved, and details how to tidy up the work as a finished piece (sew in and cut loose threads, iron, etc.)
- gives a timeline to complete each process
- includes risk management.

☐ Make your product, following all safety precautions, aiming for quality, re-doing where necessary, and record your production work in the journal page (of the template); insert photos, including one of the finished product, in your last journal entry, annotating any differences from your final design drawing (i.e. to explain how your finished product looks compared with how you thought it would look).

☐ Evaluate your finished product, explaining how it met the criteria for success (in the template).

☐ Evaluate the production process (attach to your template), explaining what processes you learnt, any trials that helped, what you enjoyed, what was difficult about working with pre-used material and planning around it, and what could be done next time to make the task more successful.

LEARN ABOUT DENIM

1 Research the type of weaving called 'twill'. Draw and annotate an enlarged diagram in the space to show how the **warp** and the **weft** are organised. Alternatively, use strips of paper in two different colours such as blue and white. The strips should be less than 10 mm wide and approximately 150 mm long. You will need at least 10 strips of each colour. Create a twill weave, paste it into the space below and add to your project template.

2 Conduct your own research to answer the following questions:

a Where does the word 'denim' originate? ....

b What is denim traditionally made of? ....

c What can denim be made of this century? ....

d What is natural indigo? ....

e What are some problems with dying jeans with synthetic indigo?

....

....

....

ANALYSIS OF JEANS

1 Consider how many pairs of jeans you own and how often you wear each pair. Ask four other people how many pairs of jeans they own and how often they wear each pair. Create a small graph. Make it visually interesting by using icons, as in the example below. Ask people what they will do with their jeans when they no longer want to wear them.

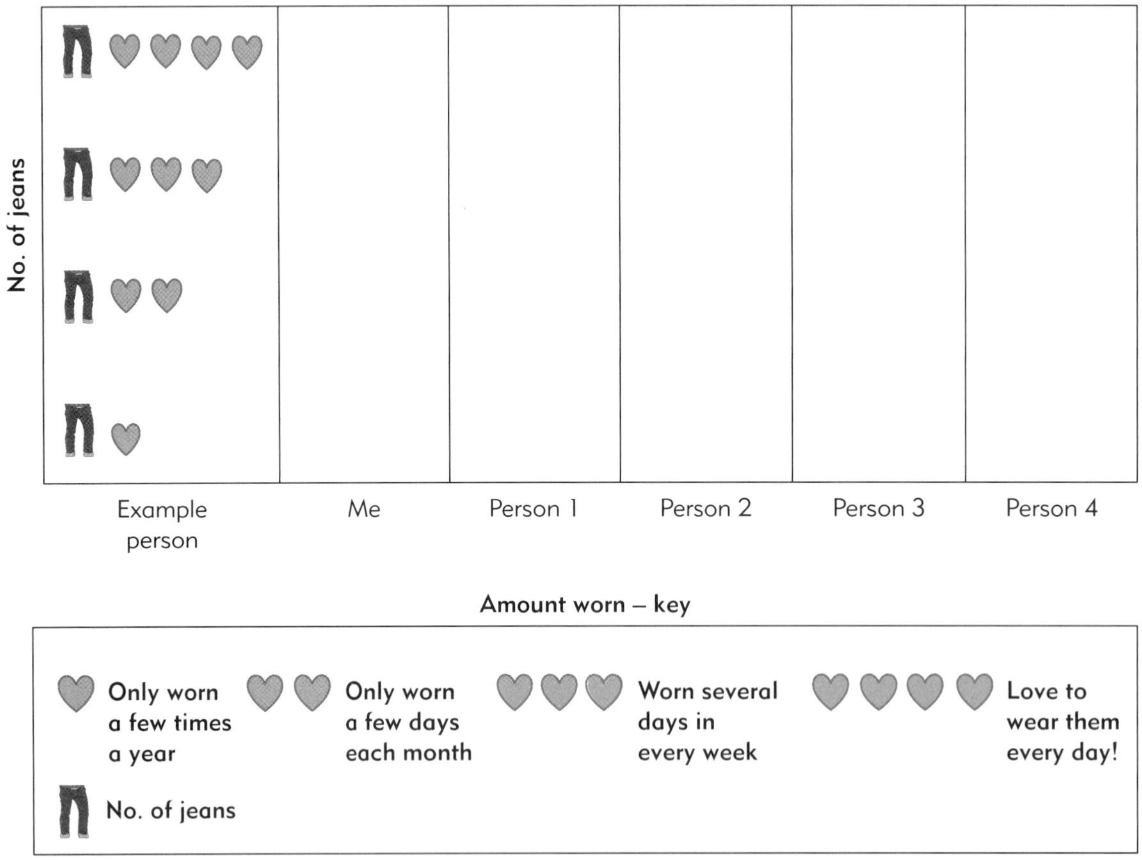

No. of jeans

Example person	Me	Person 1	Person 2	Person 3	Person 4
4 hearts					
3 hearts					
2 hearts					
1 heart					

Amount worn – key

Only worn a few times a year (1 heart)

Only worn a few days each month (2 hearts)

Worn several days in every week (3 hearts)

Love to wear them every day! (4 hearts)

No. of jeans

2 Take the pair of jeans you intend to re-use. Use a new blank page and draw (or insert a photo of) the top section only. Annotate the 'extra' bits (waistband, belt loops, zipper, button or stud fly, side zipper/buttons, leather tag, studs, rivets, etc.) and the fibre content of the fabric they are made from (refer to the label).

Continue with the tasks (outlined at the start of the challenge) using Template A.

Use the General template (A) starting on page 129 to complete your challenge.

  9780170400206

KITCHEN GARDEN DESIGN CHALLENGE

DESIGN CHALLENGE 10.3: KITCHEN GARDEN

Work in teams to create a sustainable edible garden for your school or for a community space.

REQUIREMENTS (LIMITS OR CONSTRAINTS)

- The space or structure must hold plants.
- You must develop a system of watering and soil improvement that keeps plants growing.
- Consider the size and cost limits set by your teacher.
- Recycled materials must be used as much as possible.
- The kitchen garden should be suitable for edible plants that are available for most of the year.
- Consider the needs of your school or the community group, and how they will benefit from the kitchen garden.

Your class will be split into the following design focus groups:

Team 1: Environment – developing a landscape plan (thinking of the space/place)

Team 2: Planting structures – designing planting structures

Team 3: Plants – investigating and choosing plants

Team 4: Soil – investigating and developing a healthy soil plan

Team 5: Watering – developing a watering plan.

DESIGN CHOICES

Each of the teams will need to make decisions regarding their focus area.

TASKS

This is a **big** design challenge – herbs are an obvious choice of edible plants, but vegetables and/or fruit could also be considered. To complete it successfully, you will need to work in teams to research and develop suggestions for each different aspect of the challenge. You will need to use Template A and/or Template C on page 143 in Part Three of this workbook, as well as planning and journal writing templates pages from Template A. Your design tasks will include:

- ☐ A **mapping task** that carefully maps the area suggested for the garden (or possible areas that could be considered), including a calculation of the total surface area of the space/s.
- ☐ A **design brief** written by each group explaining the situation, and the specific needs they are researching and designing for.
- ☐ **Criteria for success**, explaining what you expect in a good solution and what part it will play in the overall project. Make sure your criteria are relevant to your team's focus and to the whole challenge.
- ☐ **Research** – relevant to your team's focus, including plants and their needs, suitable soil and soil care, watering systems, planting-bed structures, overall design (including any other features).
- ☐ **Design** sketches, design options or plans, including meetings between teams to coordinate and share ideas.
- ☐ **Planning** – steps for making and costs, and a timeline coordinating each group's input.
- ☐ Putting the plan into action – **making** your garden.
- ☐ Presentation and evaluation report.

INVESTIGATING – MAPPING THE AREA

With the help of your teacher, identify the area that will be used to create the garden.

1 As a team, draw a quick bird's-eye view sketch of the area as it is currently, then measure it and draw a scale map in the space provided (you may need to draw this on a larger grid and attach it to this page). On your map, show:

- the scale
- the boundaries of the area
- any existing structures, paths, trees, or features in and around the area
- any changes in the terrain – high and low spots
- any important features you need to be aware of for your planning; e.g. taps
- any hidden features, such as pipes (you may need to ask your teacher or the school admin staff).

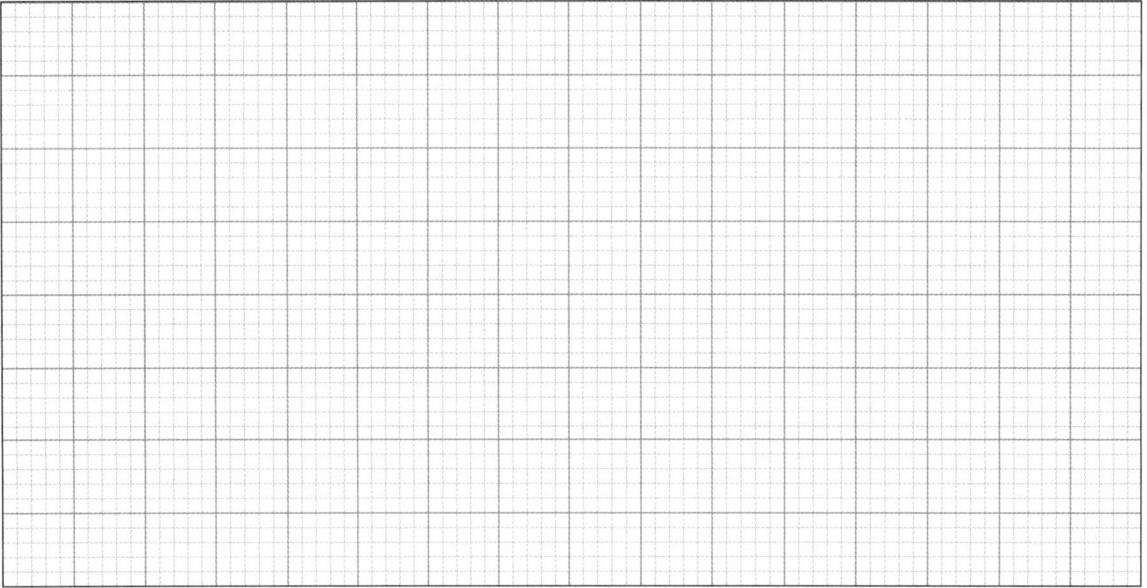

2 Talk with people who currently use the space, asking them how they might like to see it improved. List their ideas here:

....

....

3 Talk with people who might use/eat the produce from the kitchen garden, finding out what types of produce would be useful. List their responses here:

....

....

4 Are there any limitations or requirements placed on the school's maintenance and ground staff or volunteers that need to be considered? Talk with someone in this area and note down their requirements here:

....

....

  9780170400206

VERTICAL GARDENS

If your school has very little space, consider designing and making a vertical edible garden.

Shutterstock.com/uladzimir zgurski

An example of a decorative vertical garden

WRITING YOUR DESIGN BRIEF AND CRITERIA

Use the design brief in the Template C on page 144 to determine your team's focus and define who and what you are designing for. Make sure you consider the people who use the space, the produce/food needs, different ways the space can be used (growing, teaching, quiet area, etc.), safety, the use of new and recycled materials, and your budget and time limits.

RESEARCHING YOUR TEAM'S FOCUS AREA

Each team needs to research the area of the project that they have been allocated. You can split your research further between your team members (use the graphic organisers in Template A on page 7 to help you plan). Possible focus areas could be:

- **Team 1:** Overall plan – investigate the types of overall solutions others have developed for the same sort of situation, and analyse their good and 'not-so-good' features, identifying what might be possible. Also, consider added features that will make the space inviting for people (seating, paths, shade, etc.)
- **Team 2:** Bed structure design – think about the space you have for the garden, and consider the materials and structures that could be used and what composting would be suitable for the types of plants suggested. Investigate any existing solutions.
- **Team 3:** Plants – identify possible plants to grow, investigating growing seasons and care requirements, whether they need to be planted each season, costs, etc. (If researching fruit trees, research the size of the tree when it is fully grown, and find out how many years it takes to bear fruit.)
- **Team 4:** Soil – find out the type of soil needed for growing healthy plants, test the current soil, and research the ways to enrich and manage the soil. Think about systems that can be used to improve the soil (e.g. composting).

- Team 5: Water systems – research different methods using a watering system and water storage, research parts and components, suitability, costs and durability.

Collect and comment on your research information and data, and attach it to your template's research page.

DEVELOPING DESIGN IDEAS

- Use the template sketch page to develop your team's design ideas. Some teams could write lists of suggestions (e.g. plant lists), others could sketch their plans or product ideas.
- Share your ideas with others in your team, and decide on a preferred direction.
- Team 1 will need to collaborate with all of the teams to get a sense of the parts that will make up the overall plan.
- Use the design option page to draw or plan one preferred concept. Use the planning or drawing skills that suit your focus area (e.g. garden plan drawing for Team 1, orthogonal drawing for Team 2, a map/flow chart for Team 4.). As a team, draw this concept on a large piece of paper and present it to the class. Make sure you use colour, line and shape effectively if you are drawing plans or products.

PLANNING AND MAKING YOUR GARDEN PRODUCTION

- Use the timeline planning template on page 154 to list the steps that need to be carried out for your focus area to be completed/made. Teams might need to work together, as some areas will take more time than others, and some may need to be completed before others can be started (e.g. the planting team might help the structure building teams). Make sure that you think about safety when planning.
- Discuss your plans with your teacher, who will have a good overview of the project and might suggest some improvements or changes.
- Use the template on page 134 to cost your plans.
- Follow your plan to create your kitchen garden. Take photos and use your journal on page 135 to record your experiences.

LAUNCH YOUR NEW GARDEN

Plan and run a garden launch, either at the end of making your new garden or when your plants are being harvested. Invite teachers, parents and friends to celebrate the great work you have done. You can even ask your principal to cut a ribbon!

At the event, get some feedback from the people who attend. In the table on the following page, write questions that cover some of the following areas to evaluate what your garden visitors think about your garden:

- How might you use the garden space?
- Will it be good for growing what is needed? Do you think it will function well?
- Are all the parts (garden beds, watering system, added features such as seats, etc.) well integrated?
- Is it an inviting space? Does it look interesting and attractive?
- Do you think it will be safe?

Add specific questions that evaluate aspects of your team's focus area. Ask at least three people your questions and record their responses in the table. Use their feedback to help evaluate your team's contribution to the kitchen garden project.

QUESTIONS	RESPONSES

Use pages from the General template (A) start on page 129 or the Group work template (C) starting on page 143 to complete your challenge.

MOVE-IT DESIGN CHALLENGE

DESIGN CHALLENGE 11.1: MOVE-IT

Design a model of a public transport vehicle to move people or goods around a city in the future.

REQUIREMENTS (LIMITS OR CONSTRAINTS)

- You need to choose from the materials specified by your teacher (or provide materials from home, such as recycled items).
- Sustainability must be considered – think of shapes or forms that will accommodate the way the model will be powered (such as where batteries or solar panels might fit), or that will allow it to move with the least amount of wind resistance.
- Size limits will be set by your teacher.
- Your model must have a futuristic aesthetic or style, which can be achieved by the shape and form, colour combinations, interesting use of line, textures, and the careful consideration of positive and negative space.
- Include one special feature (such as access for wheelchairs, or a method to transport baggage on a bicycle).
- Focus on the design of the exterior – don't be too concerned about the interior.

DESIGN CHOICES

You will need to make decisions regarding:

- the space your vehicle travels in, and how it will be powered
- materials to use
- the shape and form of your model, and how to achieve a futuristic aesthetic
- the methods you will use to construct your model, or to 3D-print its parts
- how it will be powered to make it sustainable.

TASKS

To complete the Move-it challenge, you need to carry out a range of design tasks. These can be done using Template A on page 129 in Part Three of this workbook. More information can be found in Chapter 11 of the *Tech by Design* Student Book.

Ask your teacher what tasks should be included from the list below (use this as a checklist – tick as you complete each task):

- ☐ In groups, discuss and brainstorm different possibilities for this challenge (i.e. mass people mover, single rider, short distance, long haul, speedy, slow, underground, ground level, above ground or in the sky), and the future time period – set a five-minute limit, and refer to page 229 of the *Tech by Design* Student Book for ideas.
- ☐ Idea transfer activity (next page).
- ☐ A graphic organiser (in Template A or Activity 1.6 on page 7) to help you define the details of your challenge, including the sustainability requirements (change the template text if needed), and how the group will work together or assign roles.
- ☐ A design brief (in Template A) with four 'criteria for success' (see the *Tech by Design* Student Book, page 230).

- [ ] Research (in template and annotate):
  - sizes of batteries or solar panels, if being used
  - information on materials for your model
  - images of futuristic designs to inspire.
- [ ] Idea sketches and notes (in your template) on: the exterior form of your vehicle; the size, form and placement of technology (batteries, sensors or solar) casings; the amount of room for the passengers/rider/goods; how your vehicle will move (wheels or a new way of moving); the materials that can be used.
- [ ] Identification of the best idea (in your template) and an explanation why.
- [ ] Work plans to construct or 3D print the model safely and a timeline with the due date.
- [ ] Construction or 3D printing of your model, following safety instructions, with photos and feedback (in your template).
- [ ] Evaluate by presenting your finished model to the class, explaining how it met the criteria for success, showing important stages of your progress, decisions that you made, and why this idea should be developed (write this out in the template first).

IDEA TRANSFER

The Superbike was developed in 1996 for Olympic cycle racing, and was a fusion of ideas from aeronautics (the science of aircraft). It had a narrow one-piece frame made from carbon fibre, and airfoil cross-sections shaped to reduce wind drag. It helped the riders break Olympic records, but is no longer used as the rules were changed to disallow such innovations. You can research the Superbike further if you want to find out more.

A view of the GT Superbike 2 (USA) from the side, 'elbow rests' and the airplane shaped handle bars.

1 Annotate the photo of the GT Superbike 2 to show all the features that contributed to making it faster, and to indicate the influence of aeronautics keeping in mind that it was much narrower than other bikes.

2 Use a dictionary or search online to find the meaning of:

a airfoil ....

....

....

b wind drag ....

....

....

c aerodynamics ....

....

....

3 Use the space below to draw:

a any aeronautical or aerodynamic features that you know of in vehicles (e.g. wings, tails, body shape)

b other ideas from aeronautics that could be used in your future transport model.

AERONAUTICAL OR AERODYNAMIC FEATURES:	OTHER IDEAS:

3 a Use the space below to draw some conventional window shapes in vehicles, houses and other buildings.

b Use the design principle of space, both negative and positive, to play around with these ideas to make them look more futuristic. For example, concentrate on the space around a window to inform the window's shape.

A CONVENTIONAL WINDOW SHAPES:	B FUTURISTIC DESIGN:

Use pages from the General template (starting on page 129) or the Group work template (page 143) to complete your challenge.

CHALLENGE 11.2

CONNECT-IT DESIGN CHALLENGE

DESIGN CHALLENGE 11.2: CONNECT-IT

Design and communicate a public transport system for the future in your state, city or neighbourhood.

REQUIREMENTS (LIMITS OR CONSTRAINTS)

- You must show an actual map of the area you are connecting, including notable landmarks (significant or important places that most people would know).
- You must include at least three different modes of transport that are sustainable.
- Modes of transport should not all move at ground level.
- The modes of transport must connect at points for passengers to transfer (be picked up or set down).
- A 3D image of a connecting point (a point for picking up and setting down passengers, such as a bus stop or airport) that would help lone commuters feel safe. Ask your teacher if you need to include this aspect.
- You must communicate one expected standard of behaviour (or behaviour not tolerated) by users of this future system.

DESIGN CHOICES

You will need to make decisions regarding:

- how to represent the mapped area your system will connect (you will probably need to distort the scale and true positions of landmarks)
- the colours and icons to use for different routes, modes and travel spaces
- features of the connection point
- the font to use and hierarchy of information (the size of different types of text to show importance and catch attention)
- how to communicate simply and clearly
- the final presentation format (poster, PowerPoint, website, brochure, stickers, etc.).

TASKS

To complete the Connect-it challenge, you need to carry out a range of design tasks. These can be done using Template A on page 129, or a combination of other templates in Part Three. More details can be found in Chapter 11 of the *Tech by Design* Student Book.

Ask your teacher what tasks should be included from the list below (use this as a checklist – tick as you complete each task):

- ☐ In groups, discuss and brainstorm different possibilities for this challenge (i.e. the mapped area and different modes to be connected, landmarks, the space modes move in, connecting points and behaviour standards) – set a five-minute limit, and refer to page 229 of the *Tech by Design* Student Book for ideas).
- ☐ Activity about transport modes (next page).
- ☐ A graphic organiser (in your template) to help define the details of your challenge (change the template text if needed) and how the group will work together or assign roles.
- ☐ A design brief (in your template) with four 'criteria for success' (see the *Tech by Design* Student Book, page 230).

- [ ] Research (in template and annotate):
  - existing maps of the area
  - notable landmarks
  - a variety of public transport maps for inspiration
  - a survey on transport users' frustrations or suggestions, and how they feel at pick-up points.
- [ ] Idea sketches and notes (in your template) on your design role (i.e. abstract maps to represent the area, landmarks and pick-up points; colour codes for each transport mode, and connections; a design of a pick-up point; signs regarding behaviour; fonts to use; where to display information).
- [ ] Identification of the best idea/s (in your template), an explanation of what it will be (i.e. map, model, brochure, poster, digital presentation) and what it will communicate.
- [ ] Work plans to produce the information, or to construct or 3D print miniature models safely and by the due date.
- [ ] Final presentation piece or models, following safety instructions, with photos and feedback on how well it communicates (in your template).
- [ ] Evaluate as a group by presenting all your finished work to the class, explaining how it met the criteria for success; complete the evaluation by seeking class feedback on what you were communicating and suggestions for improvement (write this out in the template first).

THINKING ABOUT TRANSPORT MODES

1 a In the box below, draw a rough diagram or map of how you get to school (include any walking). It doesn't have to be to scale, or in correct geographic positioning.

b Create diagrams to indicate the landmarks of your house, your school and any other significant buildings en route. Copy the icons below or create your own to represent the method of transport, colour them, and use the same colour to indicate their path or route. Draw a coloured circle for any connection or pick-up point. Give your map a heading, and indicate the time taken.

2 What are the best aspects of your school journey?

3 Do you feel better when you get to school under your own steam, i.e. walk or ride or when you go to school in a vehicle? Explain.

4 What opportunities are there for you to connect with other people on your journey to school?

5 Do you have to wait at any 'connecting points'? If so, what don't you like about this wait?

6 How could this connecting point be improved?

7 What would be your dream mode of transport to get to school?

8 Create a new icon for your dream mode.

9 Prepare for this challenge by:

- collecting as many transport maps as you can (online or hard copy)
- interviewing classmates on how they get to school/holidays, etc.
- finding out the longest wait times at connection points in between transport modes for your classmates
- getting suggestions on how to make a comfortable pick-up point that allows for social connectedness
- using your 'route to school' map to inspire the design of your transport system.

10 Present your research findings, using visual methods when possible, and continue on with the tasks for this challenge.

Use pages from the General template (starting on page 129) or the Group work template (page 143) to complete your challenge.

CHALLENGE
11.3

INSIDE-IT DESIGN CHALLENGE

DESIGN CHALLENGE 11.3: INSIDE-IT

Design and make a model of an interior aspect (such as seats, a lounge chair, storage, a bicycle rack, a tray, wi-fi, power, toilets, taps, etc.) for a future transport mode.

REQUIREMENTS (LIMITS OR CONSTRAINTS)

- Choose from the materials specified by your teacher (or provide materials from home, such as recycled items).
- Your model must have a futuristic aesthetic or style, which can be achieved by the shape and form, colour combinations, interesting use of line, textures, and the careful consideration of positive and negative space.
- Focus on the look of your model – don't be too concerned about whether the functional aspects work.

DESIGN CHOICES

You will need to make decisions regarding:

- the type of future transport you are designing for, the interior aspect and its size
- materials to use
- aesthetics to suit the end-users (achieved by shape, form, colour, texture, etc.)
- the methods you will use to construct your model or 3D print its parts.

TASKS

To complete the Inside-it challenge, you need to carry out a range of design tasks. These can be done using Template Templates A or C on pages 129 or 143, or a combination of other templates in Part Three. More details can be found in Chapter 11 of the *Tech by Design* Student Book.

Ask your teacher what tasks should be included from the list below (use this as a checklist – tick as you complete each task):

- ☐ In groups, discuss and brainstorm different possibilities for this challenge (i.e. seating, storage, bathrooms, hardware, electronics, short- or long-haul vehicle, private or public, economy or luxury class, etc.) – set a five-minute limit, and refer to page 229 of the *Tech by Design* Student Book for ideas.
- ☐ Various activities (this page and next).
- ☐ A graphic organiser (in your template) to help you define the details of your challenge and how the group will work together or assign roles.
- ☐ A design brief (in your template) with four 'criteria for success' (see the *Tech by Design* Student Book, page 230).
- ☐ Research (in template and annotate):
  - images of different transport interiors
  - a survey on transport users' frustrations, or suggestions on what they would like inside
  - sustainable materials that could be used on vehicle interiors
  - images of beautiful, futuristic-looking transport interiors.

- [ ] Idea sketches and notes (in template) for your design role (i.e. combinations of shapes, forms, colours, lines, textures, and positive and negative space, functional aspects, materials to be used etc.).
- [ ] Identification of the best idea/s (in template) and an explanation of what it will be (i.e. model or 3D printed).
- [ ] Work plans to construct or 3D print the model safely and by the due date.
- [ ] Final model, following safety instructions, with photos and feedback from the group (in template).
- [ ] Evaluate by explaining how your design met the criteria for success; complete the evaluation by seeking class feedback and suggestions for improvement (write this out in the template first).

SURVEY YOUR CLASSMATES

Create survey questions that will give you design ideas for your challenge and gather responses. You could ask: *What transport have you taken in the last week/month/year? How long was the trip and how far did you go? Were you comfortable for the whole journey? What do you like about the transport? What do you dislike about it? What would be your wish list for this type of trip? What sort of activities do you typically do on this trip? What other activities would you like to do on this type of trip?*

IMPROVING A SEAT

Think of a typical bicycle seat. Now imagine a bicycle that remains balanced at all times, no matter what movements the rider makes. Draw some ideas for a more comfortable, futuristic-looking bicycle seat for such a bicycle.

1 Draw two typical bicycle seats below, make your drawings large.

2 Draw several futuristic bike seat designs that enable specific activities.

9780170400206

MOOD BOARD

Use a single PowerPoint slide or the space below to create a mood board for your interior design. Use the colour and texture palette to depict the colour combinations you like, and to indicate different materials. Find images of interior designs you like and crop them to isolate the sections that you could use in your own design. Attach to your project.

FUTURE TRAVEL ACTIVITIES

A mind map can help you decide on what interior aspect to design. Think of all the activities you might like to do whilst travelling in transport of the future and write them in the first layer of boxes from the centre. In the next layer, write the facilities that would enable these activities.

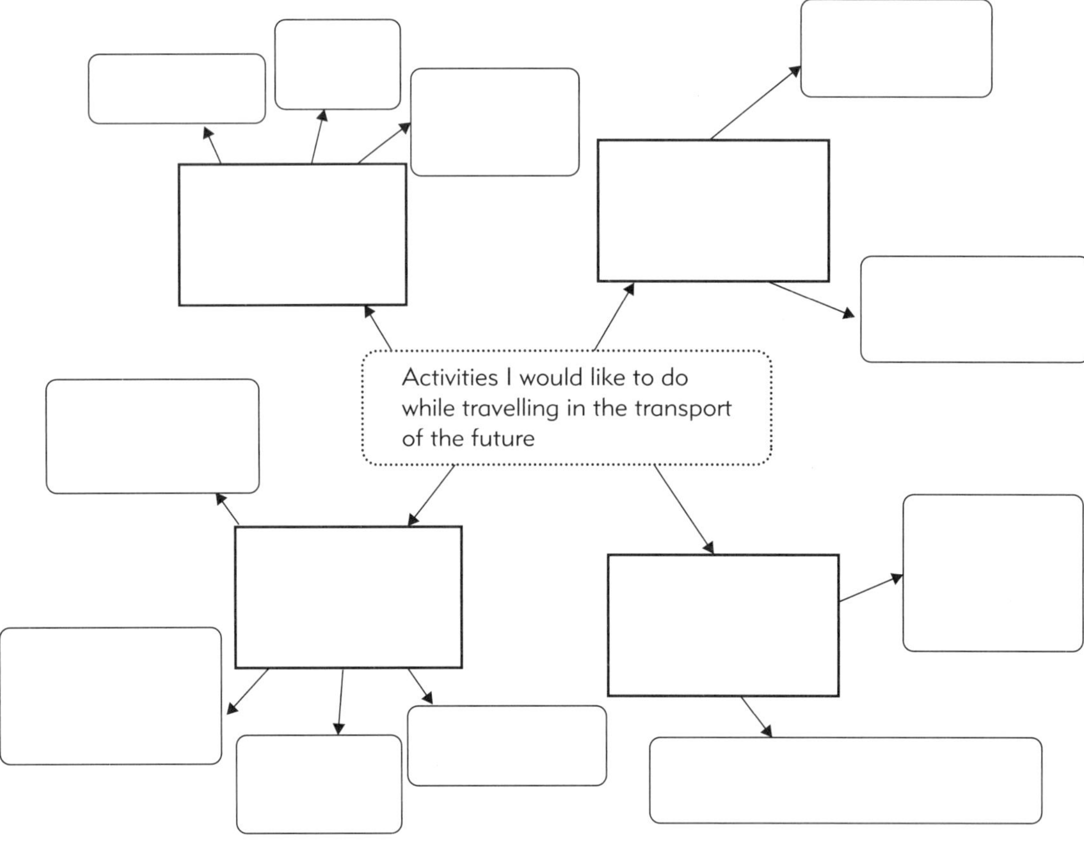

Use pages from the General template (starting on page 129) or the Group work template (page 143) to complete your challenge.

TEMPLATE A: GENERAL

You will use these templates to record the thinking, drawing, planning and evaluating you do for your design challenges. Your teacher will explain which template to use.

NAME OF CHALLENGE: ______________________

Suggest at least 4–5 possibilities for each area in the mind map below.

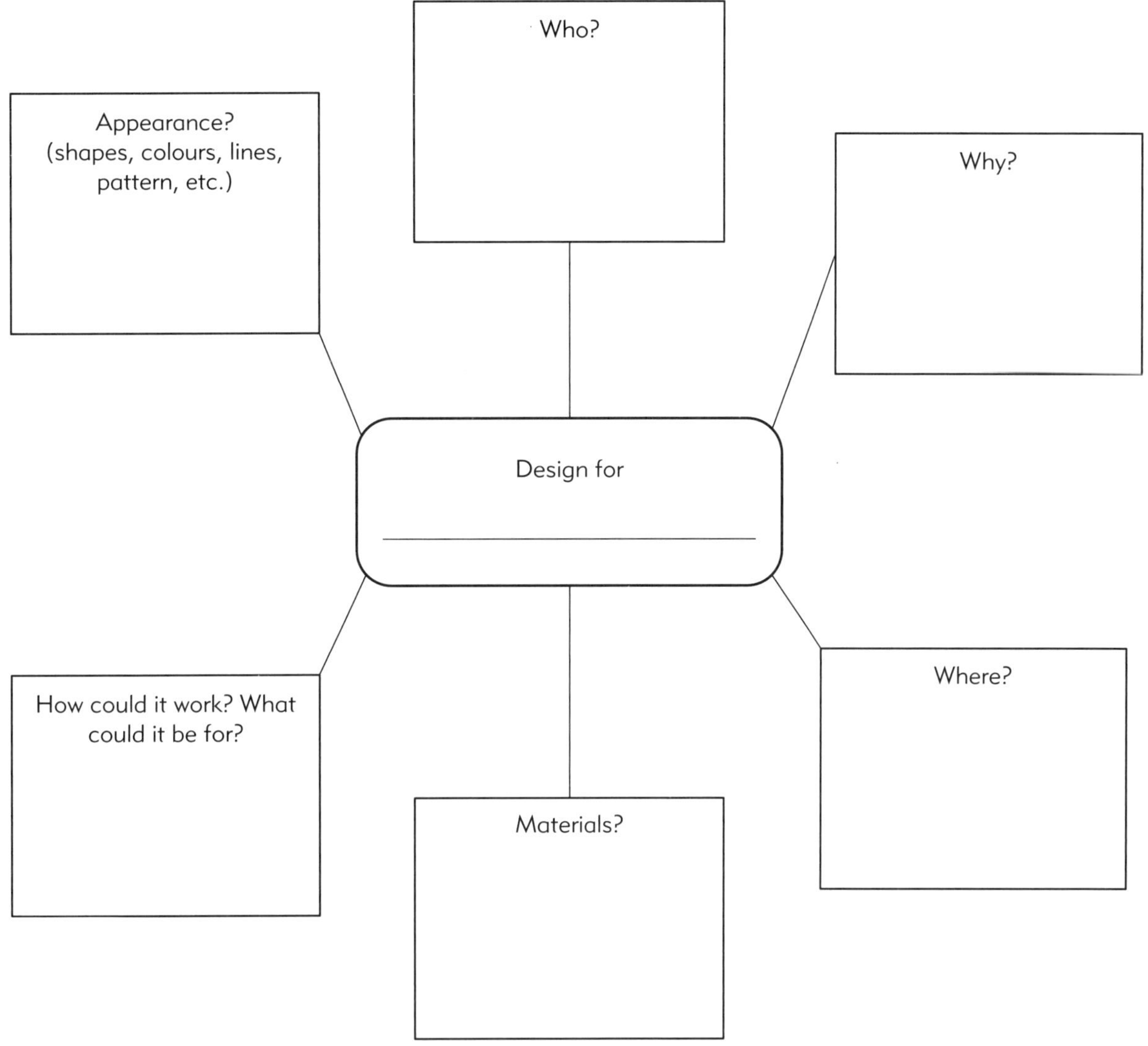

DESIGN BRIEF – EXPLAINING THE OPPORTUNITY, NEED OR PROBLEM

Highlight the best suggestion in each of the area above – include all of them in the written brief below.

I need to design and make a:

....

....

....

....

....

....

CHALLENGE: ______________________________

CRITERIA FOR SUCCESS

Write 4–6 criteria for success that explain your expectations of the finished product (your expected standards). Write your criteria as **questions** – e.g.

Does my product ....?

Is my product ....?

Complete 1–2 criteria for each of the areas below:

Function:

....

....

Construction:

....

....

Appearance:

....

....

Other (sustainability, safety, durability, etc.):

....

....

9780170400206

CHALLENGE: ______________________________

RESEARCH ON: ______________________________

You can complete research in a wide range of areas relevant to your design challenge. On the list below, tick or highlight the research you have done. Some of these research tasks are in other sections of the workbook (write down the page where your teacher can find this work); others can be completed digitally on your computer, tablet or device, or you can attach hard copies to this page. You need to complete **1–3** research tasks (as directed by your teacher).

- ☐ Inspiration (images of existing products) page ....
- ☐ The design situation (photos and observations) ....
- ☐ Surveys or questionnaires ....
- ☐ Observations of people ....
- ☐ Mood board – page ....
- ☐ Materials information – page ....
- ☐ Materials testing – page ....
- ☐ Joins research – page ....
- ☐ Decorative methods – page ....
- ☐ Finishes ....
- ☐ Trials or tests ....
- ☐ Modelling ....

TEMPLATE A: GENERAL

CHALLENGE: ______

IDEA SKETCHES FOR: ______

Using a greylead pencil, draw quick ideas in each square for your design challenge. Write comments to explain your sketches – how they work, materials, joins, etc. Add colour and/or use a fineliner on to several ideas (or around them) to make the page more exciting and so that the best features stand out.

 9780170400206

CHALLENGE: ______________________

DESIGN OPTIONS FOR: ______________________

Create two or more drawings (design options 1 and 2 on this page) that show how the whole product (model, system, solution) could look. Make your drawing 3D (where suitable), coloured and annotated to explain how it meets the criteria for success for the challenge (add comments to explain and describe).

Design option 1

Design option 2

The best design is number ....

Explain how this option fulfils your criteria for success.

....

....

....

....

....

Complete and attach a working or construction drawing if required.

TEMPLATE A: GENERAL

CHALLENGE: ____________________

PLANS

Use the space below to plan your production stages. If more detail is required, complete your production plans on a device, computer or tablet. Questions in the table on page 153 may help you.

STEPS FOR PRODUCTION	TIME	SAFETY GUIDELINES

Materials cutting list for WMP (wood/metal/plastic) products

PART	NO.	LENGTH	WIDTH	THICKNESS	SOURCE MATERIAL/COMMENTS

Complete and attach safety plans or a risk assessment if required

 9780170400206

TEMPLATE A: GENERAL

CHALLENGE: ______________________________

JOURNAL: ______________ DATE: ______________ TIME TAKEN: ______________

Answer the questions below with detailed reflections.

Pictures of work in progress

While you are making your product, take photos of your progress and of you at work, and place them here. Under each picture, briefly explain what you are doing.

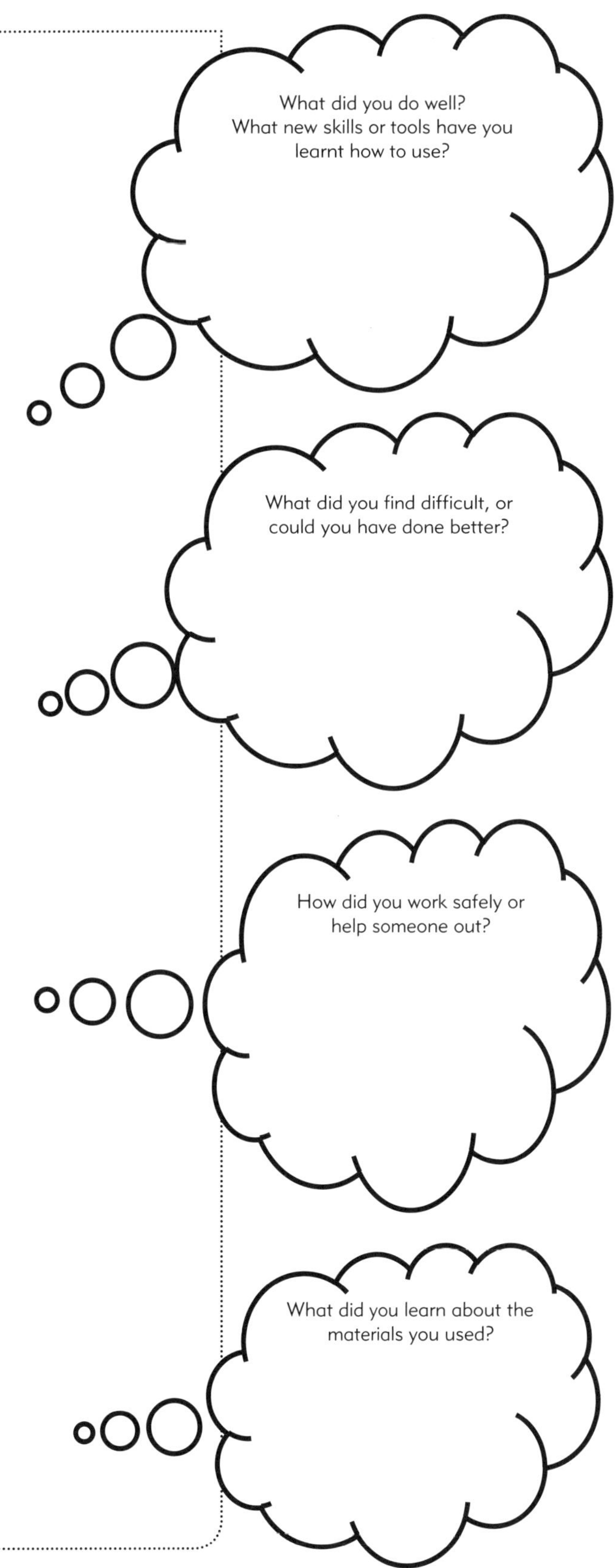

9780170400206

CHALLENGE: ______________________

PRODUCT EVALUATION

Use this evaluation activity to make judgements about how successful your finished product is.
In the left column, copy the criteria for success you wrote for your product early in the design process.
In the middle column, explain how you checked or tested this aspect (each criterion) of your product.
This could include:

CRITERIA FOR SUCCESS	HOW DID YOU CHECK THIS ASPECT?	HOW WELL DID YOUR PRODUCT PERFORM IN THIS AREA?
Insert your criteria for success for the product in this column (page 130)	Examples: trying the product out in its situation; making observations; asking for feedback from people who have used it	Discuss how well your product performed in each area, being honest about its good and bad points.

 9780170400206

CHALLENGE: ______________________________

FURTHER EVALUATION OF THE PRODUCT AND PROCESS

How 'good' is your finished product – does it work, is it made well and does it look good?

What aspect of your product could you improve?

What is the best feature of your product?

Give an example of when you showed persistence during the design and production process.

How could you improve the way you worked during any of the following design and production stages?

- *brainstorming and writing your design brief*
- *investigating*
- *sketching ideas and drawing your chosen design*
- *planning materials and production*
- *making your product*
- *safety and following your plan.*

NAME OF CHALLENGE: ______________________

Follow the instructions for the challenge, and draw a graphic organiser to assist you in finalising the details of who you are making the product for, what it will need to do, and any size and cost limits.

DESIGN BRIEF

Outline the purpose of the project, the user of the product and the situation.

I need to design and make a system ('machine' or robot) that: ....

....

....

....

....

CRITERIA FOR SUCCESS

Include expectations for any mechanical or electrical parts of the product, your construction skills, the ease of use of the finished product and the final appearance of the product.

Criterion 1: ....

....

Criterion 2: ....

....

Criterion 3: ....

....

Criterion 4 (optional extra): ....

....

 9780170400206

CHALLENGE: ______________________________

RESEARCH ON: ______________________________

You can complete research in a wide range of areas relevant to your design challenge. On the list below, tick or highlight the research you have done. Some of these research tasks are in other sections of the workbook (write down the page where your teacher can find this work); others can be completed digitally on your computer, tablet or device, or you can attach hard copies to this page. You need to complete **1–3** research tasks (as directed by your teacher).

☐ Similar products – find three images of similar products. Write a short comparison.

☐ Mechanism

- insert images of each mechanism that you will use
- annotate to explain the key features
- compare two mechanisms with similar features (if required).

☐ Electronics

- insert images of each component that you will use
- give the symbol for each electrical component
- explain the function of the component
- compare two components with similar features (if required).

☐ Construction and joins research (if required)

- some products will require research into joins and construction techniques.

9780170400206

CHALLENGE: ______________________________

IDEA SKETCHES FOR: ______________________________

Using a greylead pencil, draw quick ideas in three of the squares for your design challenge. Draw the final design in the last square, use a fineliner and colour to make it look realistic.

	Final design

 9780170400206

CHALLENGE: ______________________________

WORKING DRAWINGS

Refer to your final idea on the previous page and create working drawings. Present two or more views (top, side, back or front) that show all the information to construct the product. The designs should show any mechanical and electronic systems; their placement or position and need to be **annotated** (written comments to explain its parts, how it works and its special design features).

View 1

View 2

CHALLENGE: ______________________________

PLANS

Use the space below to plan your production stages. If more detail is required, complete your plans on a device, computer or tablet, then print out and attach it to this page. Questions on p. 153 may help you.

STEPS FOR PRODUCTION	TIME	SAFETY GUIDELINES

Mechanisms and/or electronics list:

NAME	NO.	DESCRIBE THE FUNCTION OF EACH MECHANISM OR COMPONENT

9780170400206

CHALLENGE: ____________________

JOURNAL

Pictures of work in progress

While you are making your product, take photos of four to eight steps during production. Attach your photos to the boxes below. Under each picture, briefly explain what you are doing and what you learnt.

STEP 1	STEP 2	STEP 3	STEP 4

CHALLENGE: ______________________________

PRODUCT EVALUATION ACTIVITY

Use this evaluation activity to make judgements about how successful your finished product is.
In the left column, copy the criteria for success you wrote for your product early in the design process. In the right column, discuss how well your product performed in each area, being honest about its good and bad points.

CRITERIA FOR SUCCESS	HOW WELL DID YOUR PRODUCT PERFORM IN THIS AREA?

HOW 'GOOD' IS YOUR FINISHED PRODUCT – DOES IT WORK, IS IT MADE WELL AND DOES IT LOOK GOOD?	WHAT ASPECT OF YOUR PRODUCT COULD YOU IMPROVE?

TEMPLATE C: GROUP WORK

NAME OF CHALLENGE: ______________________

DISCOVERY MAP – EXPLORING PEOPLE'S SITUATION AND NEEDS

After research and discussion with your team or classmates, complete the boxes on this page that are relevant to your design challenge and its requirements.

What specific needs are you designing a solution for?

In this area of need, what is the current situation like (from your reading and observation)? How do the people manage?

Who are you are designing for?

Provide details – age, location, name of community, etc.

What are the issues or problems with this? Why do they need a new solution?

What constraints or limits do they have?

What does the new solution need to do? Any definite requirements?

Is there any background information that might have an impact on design decisions?

What opportunities or new possibilities are there?

CHALLENGE: ______________________________

DESIGN BRIEF

Situation (the background story) focussing on the people, their current circumstances and their needs: Who is involved? Where are they? Why is a solution needed – what is the issue? What does the solution need to do? When is it needed, or when will it be used?

E.g. Toni and Jon live in a remote country town and are having problems with ....

Or — The young children in the village community of ....

- What type of product or solution is required?

- What are the limitations of the people and the constraints of situation?

- What do you need to research further? What information/observations/discussion do you need?

CRITERIA FOR SUCCESS

List 4-5 criteria that explain what you expect of, or need from, the finished product/solution so that it suits the needs of the people using it. *Explain the strategies you will use while developing your design to make sure your product meets the criteria.*

CRITERIA	STRATEGIES TO MAKE THIS HAPPEN
■	■ ....
■	■ ....
■	■ ....
■	■ ....
■	■ ....

CHALLENGE: ____________________

RESEARCH FOR DESIGN

You can complete research in a wide range of areas relevant to your design challenge. On the list below, tick or highlight the research you have done. Some of these research tasks are in other sections of the workbook (write down the page where your teacher can find this work); others can be completed digitally on your computer, tablet or device, or you can attach hard copies to this page. You need to complete **1–3** research tasks (as directed by your teacher).

- ☐ further research into the situation and people (observation and discussions, if possible)
- ☐ researching existing solutions, possible alternatives or new technologies (if relevant)
- ☐ materials research
- ☐ experiments, trials and tests
- ☐ other (explain).

IDEA SKETCHES FOR: ____________________

Using a greylead pencil, draw quick ideas in each square for your design challenge – comment on how it works, materials to be used and how it might be constructed.

■ Identify which design idea will best suit the people and the situation.

■ Explain why?

CHALLENGE: ____________________

MODEL OR PLAN

Work by yourself or in a group to create a large plan or model of your design – this can be 2D or 3D. Take a photo of it, print and attach it to this page. Identify and comment on the main features of your design or model – what you think will work well, how you have addressed specific needs or issues, what you are unsure of, etc. Aim to get at least two comments from all group members, or from several classmates if you are working by yourself.

NOTE

If you are going to make a real version of this model or design, use the planning pages and journal from design templates 1 or 2 to help you plan and make your designed solution, and to reflect on your progress.

EVALUATION REPORT

When your project is finished, discuss each aspect with your group or another class member if working individually. Use your criteria to assess and make judgements about your solution to the challenge.

CRITERIA	WHAT STRATEGIES DID YOU USE DURING DEVELOPMENT?	HOW WELL DOES YOUR SOLUTION SATISFY THIS CRITERIA?	RATE OUT OF 5
			/5
			/5
			/5
			/5
			/5

How successful is your solution? Explain why?

....

....

....

....

  9780170400206

CHALLENGE: ______________________________

How would this product/environment improve the lives of the people it is designed for?

Were there major limitations, issues or problems that made it difficult to design for this situation? Were there areas of information/research that were hard to investigate? Explain.

Do you think it would be difficult to make the product from your plan or model? What extra work would need to be done?

If you made the product/solution, how difficult was it to produce?

For a group project: How well did you work as a team? How could you improve your teamwork?

If you made your product/solution, what feedback have you been given from those using it? What can you observe about how the solution is being used, and how successful it is?

9780170400206

Additional Template pages can be combined with other templates to complete the design process.

NAME OF CHALLENGE OR PROJECT: ______________________

DESIGN BRIEF – EXTENSION

Outline:

What problem are you solving, or opportunity are you creating for? (Avoid using the name of the intended product).

....

....

....

Who will use your product? Where will they use it, and when and how often will they use it?

....

....

....

Do they have any specific or special needs?

....

....

Function:

What does the product need to do?

....

....

....

Appearance:

What colours textures, patterns or style does the user like/dislike? (The user could be you).

....

....

Sustainability:

What areas should you think about to make sure the product is sustainable?

....

....

....

TEMPLATE D:
EXTENSION –
YEARS 9-10

CHALLENGE: ______________________________

Requirements and limits (constraints):

Size limits? ....

Due date for finished product? ....

Budget (or materials/components that can be used). ....

....

Specific requirements from the teacher or the challenge? ....

....

....

....

Criteria for success:

CRITERIA	STRATEGIES YOU COULD USE DURING RESEARCH, DESIGN AND PRODUCTION	HOW WILL YOU KNOW IF YOU ARE SUCCESSFUL?

CHALLENGE: ______________________________

MATERIALS TESTING

You can carry out a materials test to find out which material will be the most suitable for making a product.

1 Choose three materials that you think might be appropriate to make your product from. List their appearance and properties.

	MATERIAL 1	MATERIAL 2	MATERIAL 3
Name:			
Appearance:			
Properties (what is it like and how does it 'behave'?)			

2 Identify one characteristic or property that you are going to test.

....

3 Why is this characteristic or property important for your product?

....

3 How are you going to test this?

....

4 For testing to be **valid** or accurate/true, the only thing that should vary between each material test should be the material (the **variable** – the aspect that changes, in this case, the material). All of the other aspects of your testing (the **non-variables**) should be exactly the same. How are you going to make sure your testing is valid or accurate?

....

....

TEST REPORT

5 Draw (or take a photo and attach) a picture of your test set-up.

USEFUL TERMS FOR TESTING

Valid – to be valid, your test needs to be accurate, true, reliable, consistent and repeatable.
Variable – the part of your test that changes, the aspect or thing you are testing.
Non-variables – all the other aspects of the test that need to be exactly the same and consistent.

 9780170400206

CHALLENGE: ______________________________

6 Record your results here – you may have to record data at different times, or you may need to repeat the test to make sure your data is consistent. Record your observations too.

RESULTS	MATERIAL 1	MATERIAL 2	MATERIAL 3	OBSERVATIONS
Test data 1				
Test data 2				
Test data 3				

7 Show your information in a graph

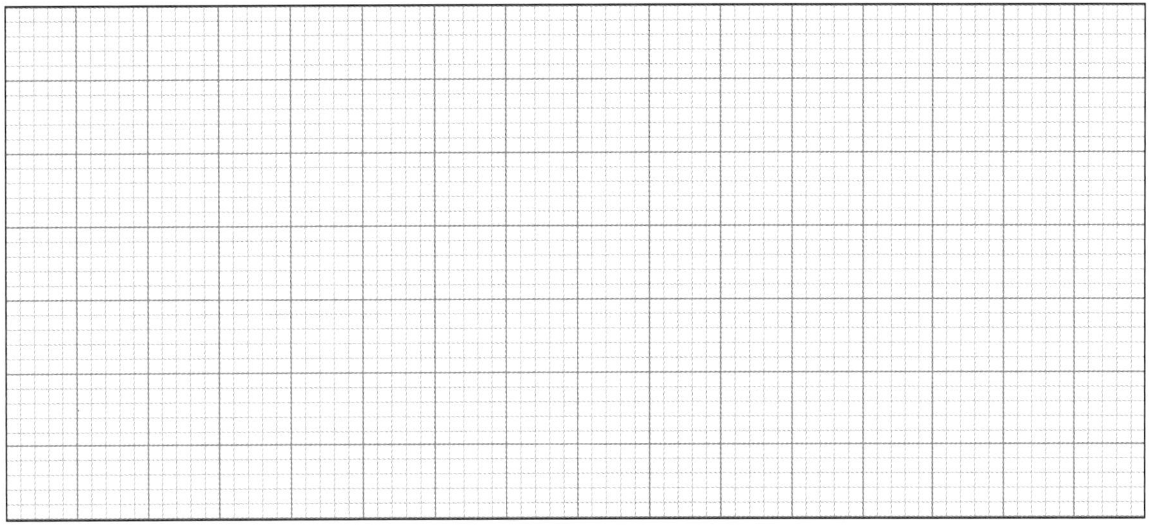

8 What does this information tell you about each of the materials you tested?

....

....

9 Which material would be the best choice for your product? Explain why.

....

....

10 a Was your test valid (accurate, reliable)? Explain why, or why not.

....

....

b How could you improve your test?

....

....

CHALLENGE: ____________________

WORK PLAN STEPS WITH ESTIMATED TIME

Describe the steps involved in making your project, and place them in a logical order. Only include the steps that are relevant, and estimate (guess) the amount of time needed to complete each one.

STEP	DETAILED DESCRIPTION OF THE STEP	RESOURCES AND EQUIPMENT REQUIRED (WHAT WILL YOU USE TO DO THIS?)	TIME NEEDED	DATE EXPECTED
Preparing the material: name the material. Does it need to be washed/cleaned? Straightened? Check that it is square, identify defects, etc.				
1.				
Measuring: what will you be measuring? Name the pieces and parts.				
2.				
Marking (or placing pattern pieces on material): what pieces will be marked? Name them.				
3.				
Cutting (or shaping) material: what pieces will be cut? Name them.				
4.				
5.				
Decorating (may need to be done later): how will any decoration be carried out.				
6.				
Joining (include all joins): name all the joins, components or items to be attached and the pieces involved. Include assembly steps.				
7.				
8.				
9.				
Finishing: what steps do you need to sand, varnish, paint, iron, trim, etc.				
10.				
Total time expected:				

 9780170400206

CHALLENGE: ____________________

TIMELINE OR GANTT CHART

On this chart, list the steps you need to complete to make your product in a logical order. Use the following steps as a rough guide: marking out, cutting and shaping, joining parts, creating fine details and decorations, assembly, and finishing (depending on your materials). Then, colour in the section showing when these steps should be completed. Use as many weeks/columns as you have available (ask your teacher). Remember, this is a plan – so complete this chart **before you start production**.

STEP	WEEK 1	WEEK 2	WEEK 3	WEEK 4	WEEK 5	WEEK 6	WEEK 7	WEEK 8	EXTRA IF NEEDED	
DATE										
1.										
2.										
3.										
4.										
5.										
6.										
7.										
8.										
9.										
10.										

CHALLENGE: ______________________________

RISK ASSESSMENT

Complete a risk assessment for the three most dangerous/risky processes or pieces of machinery you need for production. For your risk assessment, you need to:

1 List the **process or machine** that is dangerous and explain how it will be used.

2 Identify the aspects of the process or machine that are a **hazard** (e.g. electrical cord, blade, etc.).

3 List the types of **injuries** that might be caused by these hazards.

4 Work out the **level of risk**.

5 List the **safety guidelines or controls** you need to follow to reduce the possibility of accidents and injuries.

1. THE PROCESS OR MACHINE	2. HAZARDS	3. POSSIBLE INJURIES	4. RISK LEVEL (1–5)	5. SAFETY CONTROLS OR GUIDELINES

9780170400206

CHALLENGE: ______________________________

WEB EVALUATION

Use an evaluation circle to score one of your design challenge solutions against your criteria for success. Write your criteria for success in the boxes around the circle.

1 Decide (individually or with a classmate) how well your product rates against each criterion and give it a score out of five.

2 Mark your score with a dot on the circle that corresponds to the score for each criterion. The inner circle is worth 0/5 and the outer circle is worth 5/5.

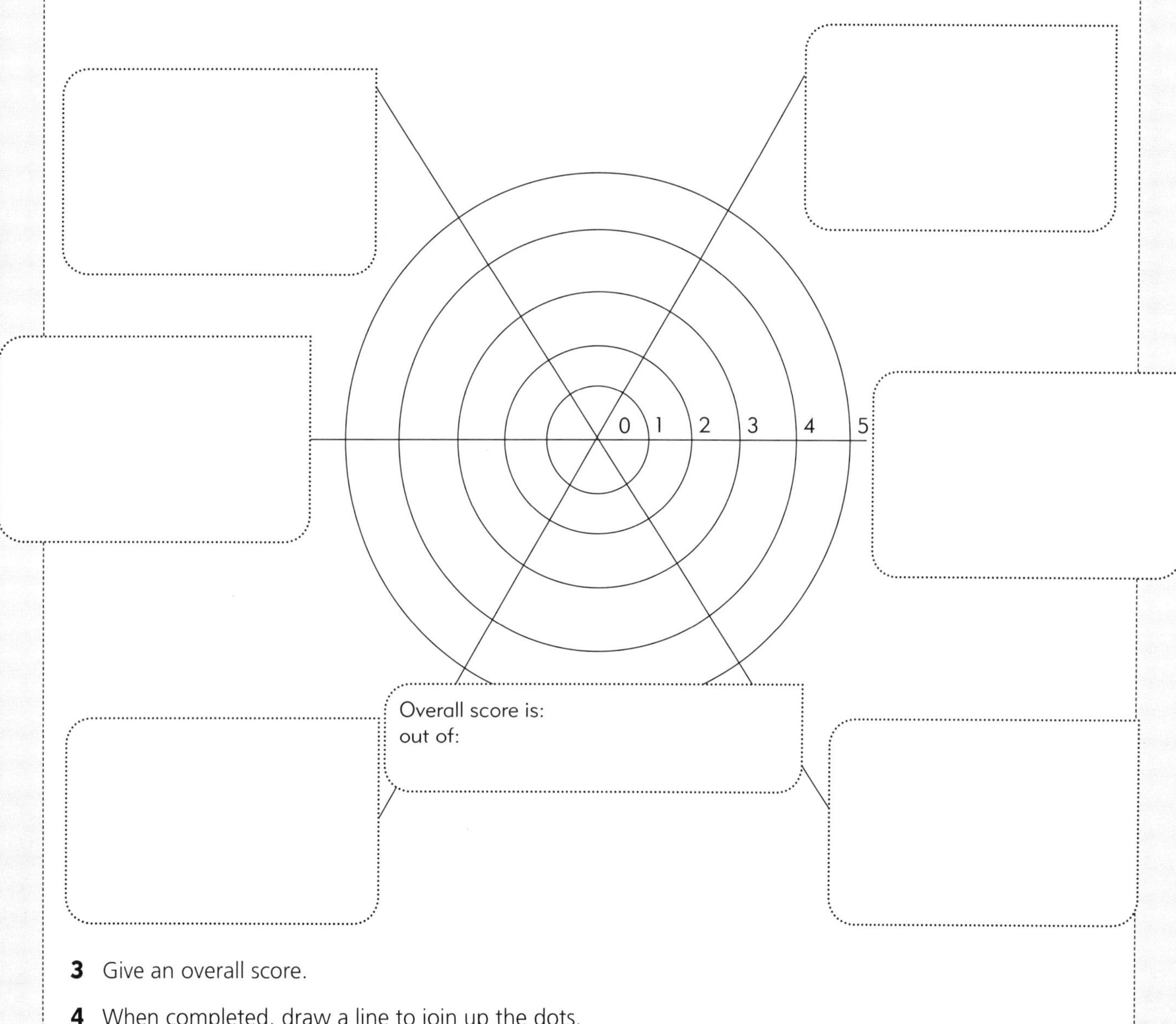

3 Give an overall score.

4 When completed, draw a line to join up the dots.

5 What improvements would you make if you did the challenge again?

....

....

....

....

TEMPLATE D: EXTENSION – YEARS 9-10

CHALLENGE: ______________________________

ENTERPRISE AND MARKETING

Your design is so successful you decide to make twenty copies and sell them at your school's open day.

Follow what is known as the marketing Ps to help make your day a success.

PRODUCT What is your product? What is it for, or what does it do? What is special about it compared with similar products? Describe it glowingly and give it a name.	
PEOPLE Who is most likely to want your product? Describe them by age, interests, income, etc.	
PLACE Where is the most likely place to sell your product on the day?	
PRICE $ What do similar products sell for? What price will you ask for your product?	
PROMOTION How will you let students, parents and teachers know about the existence of your product? Will you use social media, noticeboards, the school newsletter, posters?	

ANSWERS

WORKSHEET 2.1

1 a **Soft:** easy to mould, press or fold; doesn't feel hard
Insulating: protects from cold and heat
Conductive: heat or electricity travels easily through the material
Absorbent: soaks up moisture
Brittle: easily broken
Durable: lasts a long time
UV resistant: doesn't change or become brittle after being in the sun for a long time
Flexible: easily bent without breaking

2 **Swimwear:** strong and durable, elastic/stretchy, resists chemicals, doesn't fade, dries quickly, not see-through: materials – lycra with polyester or nylon
Parkbench: strong and durable, doesn't weaken in sunlight, weather resistant, easily cleaned: materials – aluminium, stainless steel, UV resistant plastic, jarrah, teak, merbau
Instrument case: light, strong and durable, easily formed/moulded, protects from water: materials – plywood, moulded plastic, fibre glass

WORKSHEET 2.2

1 a **Fibre:** hair-like strand
b **Fabric:** cloth made from interlocking, woven or entangled threads
c **Yarn:** fibres spun together to make a thick thread

2 Left side: natural – protein and cellulose; examples will vary
Right side: manufactured – regenerated and fully synthetic (man-made); examples will vary

3 **Synthetic:** filament or strand made from manufactured chemicals
Natural: fibres that are grown naturally
Manufactured: made by people from natural or synthetic fibres
Regenerated: chemically altered fibres from nature (usually from plants)
Cellulose: comes from a plant

6 a L to R: felted, knitted, woven

WORKSHEET 2.3

1 a Outer bark
b Inner bark
c Cambium
d Sapwood
e Heartwood
f Leaves and needles
g Flowers, fruit and nuts
h Crown
i Branches and twigs
j Trunk
k Roots

2 **Softwood:** needles, cones, only evergreen; examples are pine, cypress, etc.
Hardwood: leaves, flowers and nuts, evergreen or deciduous; examples are eucalyptus, oak, beech, etc.

WORKSHEET 2.4

1 a **Ferrous:** contains iron
Non-ferrous: doesn't contain iron
Alloy: a mix of metals, sometimes with other chemicals/minerals
Plated metal: a thin layer of one metal placed over the top of another
Precious metal: a metal that is rare and highly valued

WORKSHEET 2.5

1 Over 100 years

2 Thermoplastic: can be heated and reshaped many times
Thermoset: once formed cannot be reformed through the use of heat

3 Many thermoplastics can be recycled

4 a The symbols indicate the type of plastic and are used for effective recycling
b 1 = PET, 2 = HDPE, 3 = PVC, 4 = LDPE, 5 = PP, 6 = PS

WORKSHEET 3.2

1 **First row** (L to R): try square, fabric scissors, rubber mallet, scribe
Second row (L to R): plane, engineer's vice, clothes iron, coping saw
Third row (L to R): crochet hook, hacksaw, claw hammer, pliers
Fourth row (L to R): quick-action clamp, pop-riveting tool, files, soldering iron
Fifth row (L to R): un-picker (quick-unpick), tape measure, retractable blade knife, chisel

3 a rivets, nuts and bolts
b pop riveter, spanners

4 a PVA
b epoxy resin (other options work)
c acrylic cement or solvent
d epoxy resin

WORKSHEET 3.3

Across

1 Tin snips **5** Soldering iron **8** Scroll saw **11** Vice **12** Steel rule **13** Nails **14** Portable drill **16** Calipers **18** Portable sander **20** Screwdriver **21** Jigsaw **23** Pop rivet **24** Glasses

Down

2 Steam iron **3** Pins **4** Gouge **6** Embroidery hoop **7** Rip saw **9** V block **10** Needle **15** Centre punch **17** Engraver **18** Piercing saw **19** G clamp **22** Spanner

WORKSHEET 3.6

1 Hand wheel
2 Bobbin winder release
3 Bobbin winder
4 Spool pin/thread holder
5 Stitch width control
6 Buttonhole control
7 Stitch length adjustment
8 Reverse control
9 Stitch selector

10 Tension control
11 Thread guide
12 Thread take-up lever
13 Needle
14 Fabric feed teeth
15 Presser foot
16 Bobbin case compartment
17 Presser foot lever
18 Light
19 Foot pedal
20 Drop feed control

WORKSHEET 3.8

1 L to R: rebate joint, cross halving joint, dowelled widening joint
2 L to R: soldered join, knocked-up seam, joining with nuts and bolts
3 L to R: zigzag stitched edging, French machine seam, overlocked seam
5 L to R: nail, press stud, plastic rivets, screws (self-tapping)

WORKSHEET 4.1

1 Scissors: shear
Vice: compression
Bending bar: refraction
Stretching chewing gum: tension
Wringing towel: torsion

WORKSHEET 4.2

1 **Weight on bar**
Label (L to R): effort, fulcrum, load
Lever class: 1
Mechanical advantage: no advantage
Fishing rod
Label (L to R): fulcrum, effort, load
Lever class: 3
Mechanical advantage: speed advantage
Weight on bar
Label (L to R): effort, load, fulcrum
Lever class: 2
Mechanical advantage: force advantage
See saw
Label (L to R) – two possible answers: effort, fulcrum, load or load, fulcrum, effort
Lever class: 1
Mechanical advantage – two possible answers: If the boy is the effort, force advantage. If the girl is the effort, speed advantage
Weight on bar
Label (L to R): fulcrum, effort, load
Lever class: 3
Mechanical advantage: speed advantage
Wheelbarrow
Label (L to R): fulcrum, load, effort
Lever class: 2
Mechanical advantage: force advantage
2 Lever class 2
3 Lever class 3
4 Lever class 1

WORKSHEET 4.3

1 a Input motion: rotary motion downward (moving faster)
b Rotary motion upward (moving slower)
c Change in direction and speed of rotary motion
2 a Rotary motion of handle
b Rotary motion of shaft attached to drum
c Change of speed of rotary motion
3 a Linear motion
b Linear motion
c Often changes direction and speed

WORKSHEET 4.4

1 b The machines combine to make it easier for the human to drag the boat up the beach
2

Name	Purpose
a Crank handle	Increase torque (rotary force)
b Worm gear	Works with c to increase torque (rotary force)
c Worm wheel	Works with b to increase torque (rotary force)
d Pulley system	Creates a force advantage

WORKSHEET 4.5

1 a Copper
b Plastic
c Opposes
d Electrons
e Circuit
2 a Load, power supply, closed path
b The power supply (e.g. batteries)
3 a Right-hand image
4 One possible answer: the symbols are standard across the world and can be understood by anyone speaking any language

WORKSHEET 4.6

1 a First row (L to R): motor, cell (or battery), switch
Second row (L to R): globe, resistor, LED
Third row (L to R): capacitor, transistor, diode
1 b First row (L to R): diode, capacitor, cell (or battery), resistor, motor
Second row (L to R): lamp, LED, switch, transistor

WORKSHEET 4.8

1 a 120 000 Ω tolerance 10%
b 390 Ω tolerance 5%
c 39 Ω tolerance 1%
2 a Red, red, orange (fourth colour not specified in question)
b Yellow, violet, brown (fourth colour not specified in question)

WORKSHEET 4.9

1 a The energy and material entering a system
b Changes to energy and material in a system
c How a system responds to inputs
d The energy and material leaving a system

2

Product	Input	Process	Control	Output
Toaster	Bread, electricity	Heat	Timer	Toast
Torch	Batteries	Change electricity to light	Switch	Light
House alarm	Burglar, electricity	Sense burglar	Control circuit	Alarm
Air conditioner	Temperature sensor, electricity	Cool air	Thermostat	Cool air

CHALLENGE 6.1

2 Rotary motion: an object moving in a circle or part of a circle (an arc)
Reciprocal motion: backward and forward motion in a straight line
Friction: a force that opposes motion, the result of two surfaces rubbing as they pass over one and another
Cam: a shaped wheel
Crank: arm attached to an axle

CHALLENGE 6.2

1. Cam with plate follower
2. Cam with roller follower
3. Cam with knife-edge follower
4. Plate and pushrod would rotate

CHALLENGE 6.3

1. Sketch an 80 mm pulley
2. Chain and sprockets can transmit greater torque (rotary force)
3. Cheaper and quieter, and can slip when required

CHALLENGE 7.1

1. Single-pole, single-throw
2.

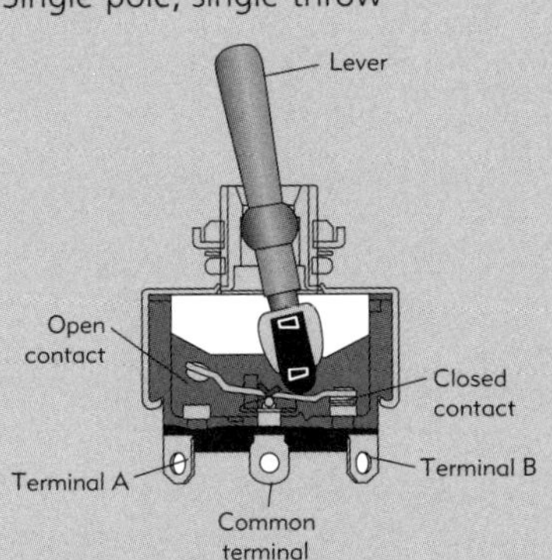

L to R: open contact, terminal A, common terminal, terminal B, closed contact

3. The common terminal must be used
4. No

DIFFERENTIAL STEERING ACTIVITY

2

Direction	Left motor	Right motor
Forward	On	On
Left	Off	On
Right	On	Off
Stop	Off	Off

3

Step direction	Left motor	Right motor	Description
1	On	On	Forward
2	Off	On	Left turn
3	On	On	Forward
4	On	Off	Right turn
5	On	On	Forward
6	On	Off	Rotate 180°
7	On	On	Forward
8	Off	On	Left turn
9	On	On	Forward
10	On	Off	Right turn
11	On	On	Forward

CHALLENGE 7.3

1. Initialises the Arduino and defines the inputs and outputs
2. Comment
3. Main section of code that continually repeats
4. Line 8
5. delay(2000);

NOTES

 9780170400206

NOTES

NOTES

 9780170400206